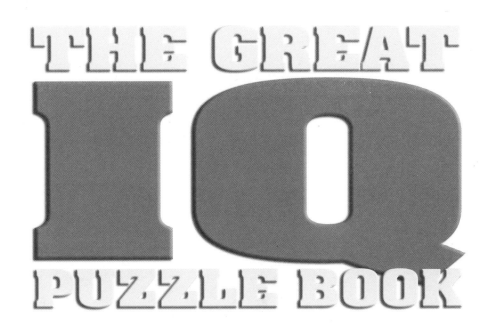

THE GREAT IQ PUZZLE BOOK

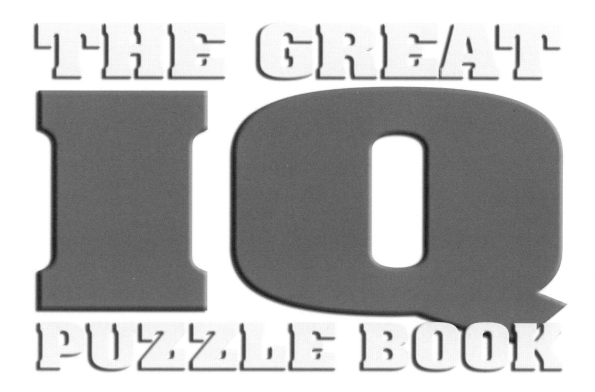

THE GREAT IQ PUZZLE BOOK

Over 600 new brain-teasing puzzles

Compiled by Ken Russell & Philip Carter

The UK MENSA Puzzle Editors

Sterling Publishing Co., Inc.
New York

Library of Congress Cataloging-in-Publication Data Available

10 9 8 7 6 5 4 3 2 1

Published by Sterling Publishing Co., Inc.
387 Park Avenue South, New York, NY 10016

© Arcturus Publishing Limited

First Sterling Edition Published in 2003

Manufactured in China

ISBN 1-4027-0966-8

HOW TO USE THIS BOOK

This book consists of twenty separate IQ sections, each containing thirty questions. The sections are of approximately the same degree of difficulty. Each has a rating by which you can assess your performance.

A time limit of sixty minutes is allowed for each section. The correct answers are given at the end of the book – award yourself one mark for each correct answer. Many answers include a detailed explanation, so that you can study the question again if you found the wrong answer. You should find that this will improve your performance on subsequent tests.

Use the following table to assess your performance on each test:

Score	Rating
27–30	Exceptional
23–26	Excellent
18–22	Very good
14–17	Good
10–13	Average

HELPFUL HINT

There are a few puzzles that involve prior knowledge of modulo calculations. The following explanation should help. The mathematics we use is a decimal system based on units of 10 or another way of expressing this is 'Modulo 10'. For instance the number 100 as Modulo 10 is as follows:

UNITS:	100	10	1
NO. OF UNITS:	1	0	0

There is one 100 unit, zero 10s and zero single units i.e:
(100x1=100) + (10x0=0) + (1x0=0) = 100

The number 100 in a Modulo 7 system, however, is based on a different number of units – see below.

UNITS:	49	7	1
NO. OF UNITS:	2	0	2

(2X49 = 98) + (7X0 = 0) + (2X1 = 2) = 100

And, the number 100 in a Modulo 6 system, is:

UNITS:	36	6	1
NO.OF UNITS:	2	4	4

(2X36=72) + (6X4=24) + (4X1=4) =100

The use of a calculator is permitted and will not invalidate your score.

•1• PUZZLE

Which box **A, B, C, D** or **E** should replace the question mark?

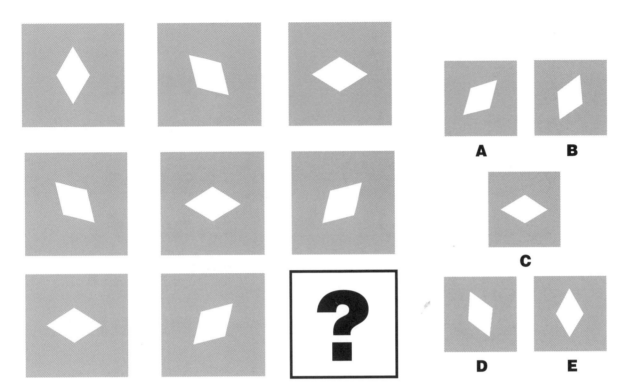

•2• PUZZLE

What letter should replace the question mark?

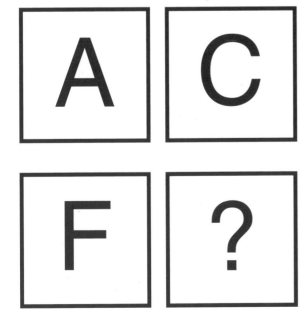

•3• PUZZLE

What number should replace the question mark?

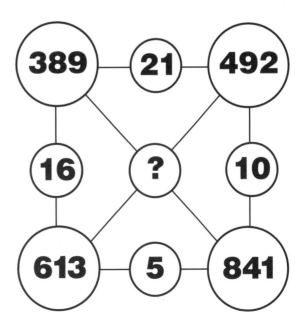

PUZZLE • 4 •

What letter should replace the
question mark?

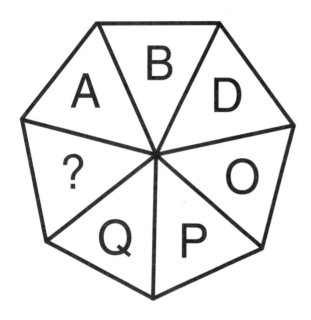

PUZZLE • 5 •

Which two words are opposite
in meaning?

Weak
Specific
Facile
Sincere
Difficult
Unreal

PUZZLE • 6 •

Which number is the odd one out?

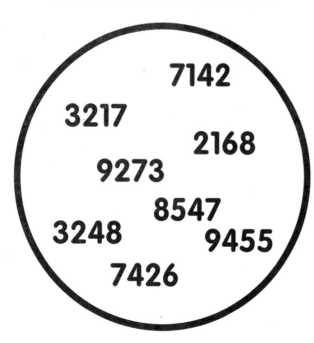

PUZZLE • 7 •

Which of the clock faces is the odd one out?

A   B   C

D   E

PUZZLE • 8 •

Which is the odd one out?

A   B   C   D   E

PUZZLE • 9 •

Ottoman is to **Seat** as **Davenport** is to:

Chair   Table   Desk   Cabinet   Mirror

PUZZLE • 10 •

Which is the odd one out?

S E C T I O N

1

• 11 •
PUZZLE

Which is the odd one out?

Semi-Breve

Treble

Minim

Crotchet

Quaver

• 12 •
PUZZLE

What number should replace the
question mark?

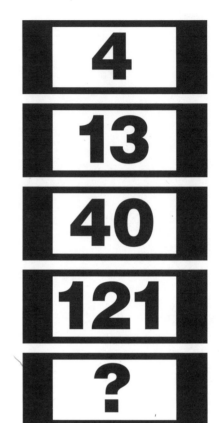

4

13

40

121

?

• 13 •
PUZZLE

What comes next?

GHKLMN

NMKHG

GHMN

?

• 14 •
PUZZLE

How many circles below contain a dot?

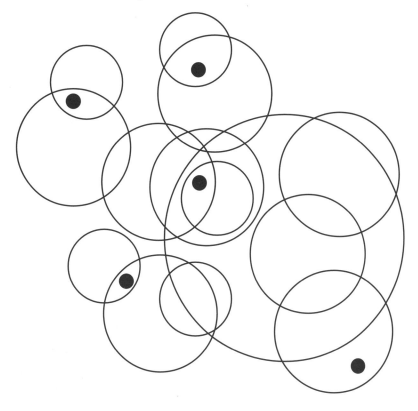

• 15 •
PUZZLE

Which two words are opposite in meaning?

Ambitious Altruistic Amenable Selfish Fraternal Tender

• 16 •
PUZZLE

What number should replace the question mark?

F	L	P	T	Q
24	4	32	4	?
D	C	B	E	J

PUZZLE • 17 •

If the score on 13 dice totals 39, what is the average of the score on the opposite sides?

PUZZLE • 18 •

What number should replace the question mark?

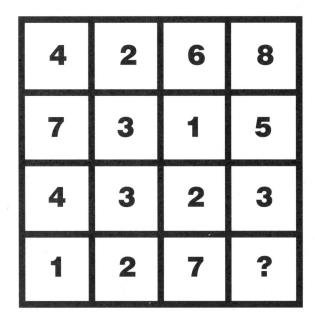

4	2	6	8
7	3	1	5
4	3	2	3
1	2	7	?

PUZZLE • 19 •

I drove my car East in a straight line for half a mile and when I stopped the car was facing West. How?

WEST   EAST

PUZZLE • 20 •

What number is two places away from itself doubled, one place away from itself plus 2, three places away from itself less 1, two places away from itself plus 5 and three places away from itself plus 7?

2	23	4	15	17
21	6	25	8	20
7	14	36	5	18
10	12	30	3	16
22	19	31	11	9

What is a Grampus?

A. Whale

B. Grandpa

C. Walrus

D. Grassy plain

E. Cat

What is the name given to a group of Wild Boars?

A. Barren

B. Clamour

C. Clutch

D. Sounder

E. Sedge

What would you always find in the Firmament?

A. Glass

B. Water

C. Stars

D. Fish

E. Numbers

What is the value of x ?

$$\frac{7}{8} \div \frac{14}{24} = x$$

S E C T I O N

1

PUZZLE

Simplify

7 - 6 x 4 + 3 ÷ 2 - 7 = x

PUZZLE

What is the curve called generating from this cut through the cone?

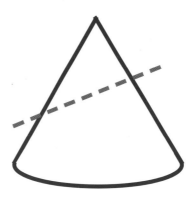

• 27 •

PUZZLE

• 28 •

PUZZLE

What comes next in this series?

0.5

0.6666

0.75

0.8

0.8333

0.8571

?

Which number should replace the question mark?

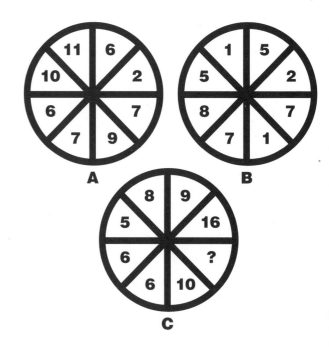

• 29 • PUZZLE

If 6 x 5 = 33

7 x 6 = ?

• 30 • PUZZLE

What number should replace the question mark?

7		6
	9	
5		3

7		13
	57	
6		3

2		9
	?	
8		4

PUZZLE 1

What replaces the question mark to complete the puzzle?

4	8	3
8	4	2
8	3	?

PUZZLE 2

Which two words are closest in meaning?

Independent

Manifest

Explain

Declaration

Evident

Multiple

PUZZLE 3

What letters should replace the question marks?

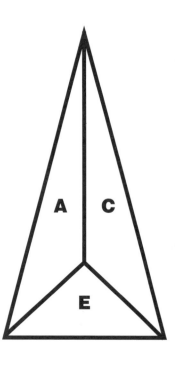
A   C

E

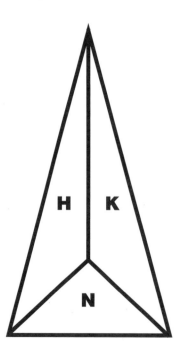
H   K

N

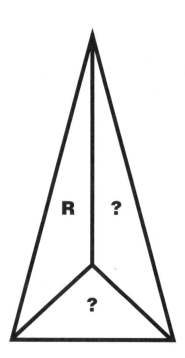
R   ?

?

• 4 • PUZZLE

What number should replace the
question mark?

3	3	4	2	11
9	3	7	8	2
12	5	5	7	1
4	2	15	6	5
10	?	3	1	5

• 5 • PUZZLE

What number should replace the
question mark?

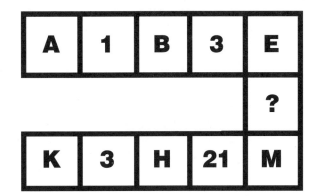

A	1	B	3	E
				?
K	3	H	21	M

• 6 • PUZZLE

Which is the odd one out?

17

• 7 •
PUZZLE

Which is the odd one out?

Femur   Fibula   Scapula   Tibia   Patella

• 8 •
PUZZLE

In this addition sum only one of the decimal places is in the correct position. Can you correct the sum by altering the four incorrect decimal points?

38.2
6.94
124.6
18.37
───────
928.36

• 9 •
PUZZLE

Acetic is to **Vinegar** as **Lactic** is to:

Powder

Milk

Soup

Fruit

Wine

• 10 •
PUZZLE

What number should replace the question mark?

74   65   61   37   58   ?

• 11 •
PUZZLE

A bag of potatoes weighs 50lbs divided by half its own weight. How much does the bag of potatoes weigh?

• 12 •
PUZZLE

What comes next in this sequence?

A   B   C   D   E   F

• 13 •
PUZZLE

What does Gregarious mean?

A. Enjoying outdoor life

B. Love of food

C. Enjoying the company of others

D. Very large

E. Very knowledgeable

• 14 •
PUZZLE

Which number is the odd one out?

526
793   382
784   329
894
932   397
478
489
652

• 15 •
PUZZLE

Which two words are closest in meaning?

Build

Edify

Act

Educate

Charm

Dictate

• 16 •
PUZZLE

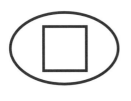 **is to**

as  **is to**

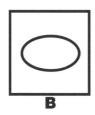 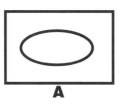 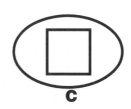 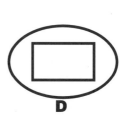 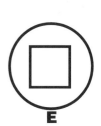

A   B   C   D   E

• 17 •
PUZZLE

369542 is to 246359

172896 is to 268179

417638 is to ?

• 18 •
PUZZLE

Which number from 1-81 appears in the grid twice, and which number is missing?

54	14	61	24	6	56	79	27	3
46	69	75	42	68	35	12	41	67
62	25	2	40	11	19	60	23	52
47	74	63	20	33	80	51	73	16
29	7	39	13	49	1	66	8	59
70	28	18	55	26	58	21	47	37
48	81	4	43	9	71	36	15	31
78	45	77	22	76	50	53	5	65
30	10	64	44	17	72	32	57	38

PUZZLE • 19 •

Which two letters should replace the question mark?

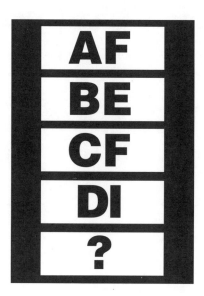

AF
BE
CF
DI
?

PUZZLE • 20 •

What letter is two to the left of the letter immediately to the right of the letter three to the left of the letter two to the right of the letter E?

A   B   C   D   E   F   G   H

PUZZLE • 21 •

Which number should replace the question mark?

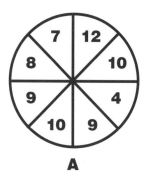

A

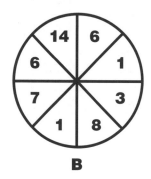

B

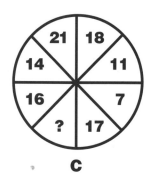

C

• 22 •
PUZZLE

Simplify

$$\frac{7}{32} \div \frac{14}{16} = X$$

• 23 •
PUZZLE

1 man can paint a fence in 2 hrs
1 man can paint a fence in 3 hrs
1 man can paint a fence in 5 hrs
1 man can paint a fence in 8 hrs

If they all worked together on the fence, each working at his same speed as before, how long would it take?

• 24 •
PUZZLE

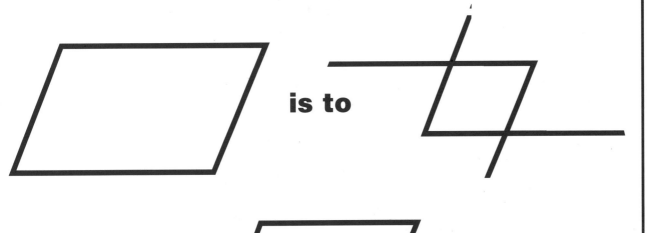

is to

as

is to

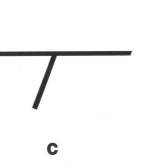

A   **B**   **C**

PUZZLE • 25 •

What is the meaning of Hydrology?
The study of...

A. Land formations
B. Water
C. Coastlines
D. Forest
E. Canals

PUZZLE • 26 •

If **Deciduous** is to **Willow** then
Coniferous is to:

A. Ash
B. Cherry
C. Fir
D. Apple
E. Lime

PUZZLE • 27 •

What is the symbol that should appear in the circle containing the question mark?
A, B, C, D or **E**?

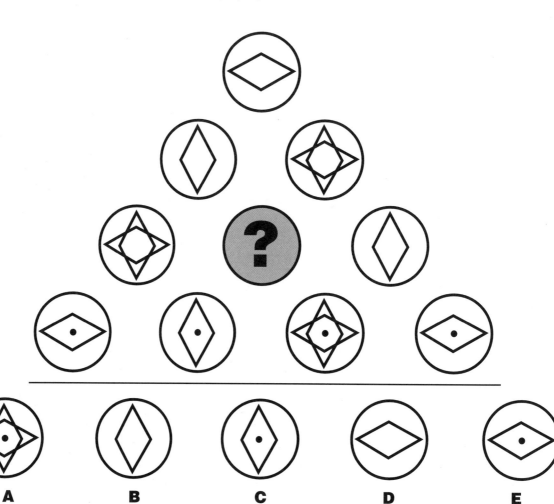

What would you always find in a Finnan?

A. Coffee   B. Haddock   C. Ginger beer
D. Cloth   E. Fishing line

What does this symbol represent?

If...

JM

KN

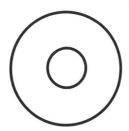

LM

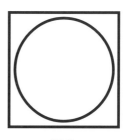

KO

What number should replace the question mark?

10   **11**   **4 ½**   **16 ½**   **-1**   **22**   **?**

PUZZLE

Tuesday is to Thursday as April is to:

May

Spring

February

Month

June

• 2 •
PUZZLE

What number should replace the question mark?

4	12	7	15
21	13	18	10
16	24	19	?

• 3 •
PUZZLE

Which letters should replace the question marks?

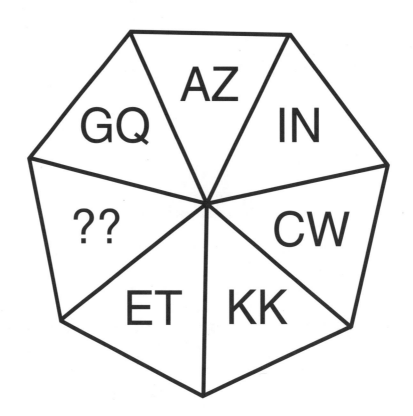

• 4 •
PUZZLE

What unusual feature is shared by the two calculations below?

$$1.5 \times 3 = 4.5$$

$$1.2 \times 6 = 7.2$$

• 5 •
PUZZLE

Which is the missing tile **A, B, C, D** or **E**?

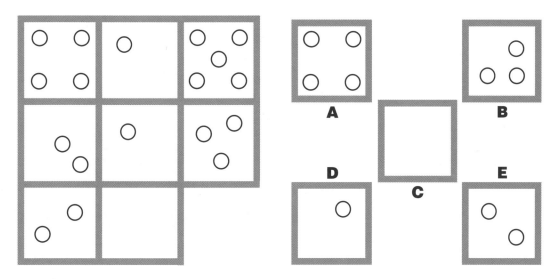

• 6 •
PUZZLE

What number should replace the question mark?

K	T	E	V	F	M
3	2	4	2	3	?

Which word in brackets is opposite in meaning to the word in capitals?

IGNOMINY (Pleasure, Honour, Knowledge, Stigma, Wisdom)

What number should replace the question mark?

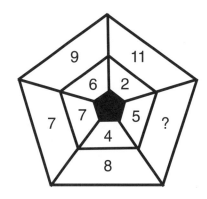

• 9 •
PUZZLE

Which is the odd one out?

Poker

Baccarat

Whist

Chess

Cribbage

• 10 •
PUZZLE

A man was born in 1969 and died in 1999 aged 73.

What is the explanation?

• 11 •
PUZZLE

To which of the boxes below can a dot be added so that the dots meet the same conditions as in the box above?

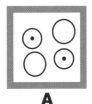

A

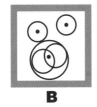

B

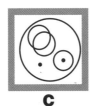

C

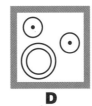

D

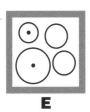

E

• 12 •
PUZZLE

Which letter should replace the question mark?

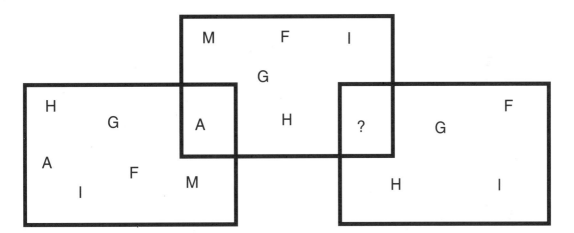

• 13 •
PUZZLE

What is Dolour?

**A. Boredom   B. African currency   C. Type of dress
D. Grief or sorrow   E. Obedience**

Which letters should replace the question marks?

H		R		B
J		T		?
K		U		?
I		S		?

• 15 •
PUZZLE

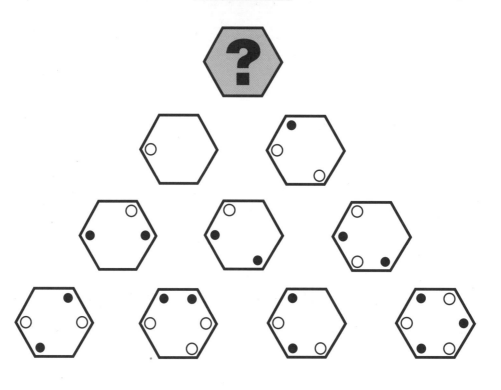

What should replace the question mark?

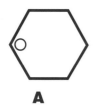 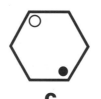 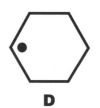 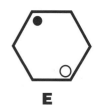

A   B   C   D   E

What value should replace the question mark?

| 4.7 | 12.1 | 13.22 | ? |

Which word in brackets means the same as the word in capitals?

INTONE (Breathe, Chant, Growl, Bear, Cry)

Which number should replace the question mark?

8	5	2
5	1	3

9	7	5
9	6	?

Four people are seated in a row in the dentist's waiting room. Mrs Brown is next to Mrs Green but not next to Mr Jones. Mr Jones is not next to Mr Gill. Who is next to Mr Gill?

• 20 •
PUZZLE

What letters are missing from the fifth rectangle?

A
1

CD
2

GHI
3

MNOP
4

?
5

• 21 •
PUZZLE

What are the next 2 numbers in this sequence?

212

223

242

526

272

829

?

?

• 22 •
PUZZLE

There were 200 adults living in the Wild West town. There were almost twice as many men in town as women and three times as many men as women were in prison. An eleventh of the men and a seventeenth of the women were in prison.
How many in total were not in prison?

PUZZLE • 23 •

Find the name of these 3 islands.

1 _ E _ M _ D _

2 _ O _ M _ S _

3 _ A _ E _ R _

PUZZLE • 24 •

Which letter replaces the question mark?

N = 15
D = 100
E = 101
O = 202
Y = 30
X = 36
? = 44

PUZZLE • 25 •

Which number replaces the question mark to complete the sequence?

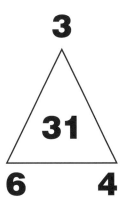

3
31
6   4

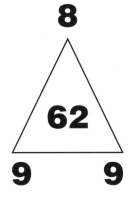

8
62
9   9

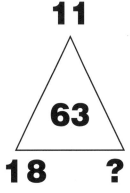

11
63
18   ?

PUZZLE • 26 •

Which circle is nearest in content to A?

A

B

C

D

E

S
E
C
T
I
O
N

3

33

PUZZLE

If 4 x 4 = 20

6 x 6 = ?

PUZZLE

What word is suggested below?

TUNE
TUNE
TUNE
TUNE

• 29 •
PUZZLE

At the local tennis club members entered a competition.

	MEN	**WOMEN**
Men's singles	36	
Women's singles		21
Men's Doubles	18 prs	
Women's Doubles		8 prs
Mixed Doubles	20 prs	

They were knockout matches, reducing to 32-16-8-4-2-1-Winner by using byes.

How many matches were played?

Which circle **A, B, C, D** or **E** fits into the blank?

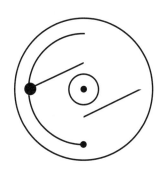
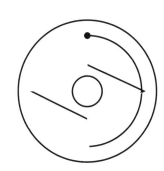
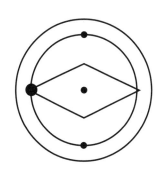

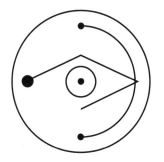
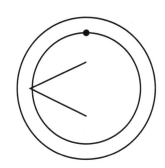

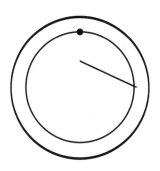
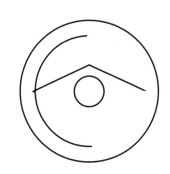
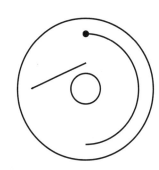

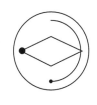

A   **B**   **C**   **D**   **E**

PUZZLE

In a recent by-election a total of 9469 votes were polled. The Liberal was elected by a majority of 749 over the Socialist, by 861 over the Conservative and by 2461 over the Independent. How many votes were cast for each candidate?

• 2 •
PUZZLE

What number should replace the question mark?

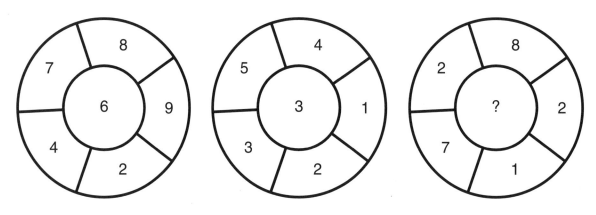

• 3 •
PUZZLE

Which four letters are missing?

A	K	J	T	L	A
K	A	L	T	J	K
J	T	L			J
T	J	K			T
L	A	K	J	T	L
A	L	T	J	K	A

A	T
J	K

A

A	K
A	L

B

A	J
L	A

C

A	T
A	L

D

PUZZLE 4

Which two words are opposite in meaning?

Credence

Error

Disbelief

Religion

Knowledge

Sorrow

PUZZLE 5

How many minutes is it before 10 AM, if fifty minutes ago it was four times as many minutes past 7 AM?

PUZZLE 6

Which is the odd one out?

Isosceles

Rhombus

Scalene

Equilateral

PUZZLE 7

What number should replace the question mark?

978

388

152

?

4

PUZZLE • 8 •

**A dictionary has 587 pages plus half its number of pages.
How many pages has the dictionary?**

PUZZLE • 9 •

What comes next in this sequence?

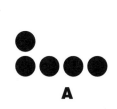 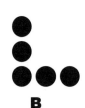 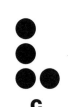 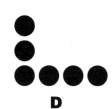 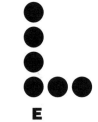

    A   B   C   D   E

PUZZLE • 10 •

Lion is to **Den** as **Rabbit** is to:

Drey

Warren

Form

Sett

Lodge

PUZZLE • 11 •

Which letters should replace the
question marks?

GP   FL   EH

JW   NT   RQ

IK   ??   UE

PUZZLE • 12 •

Which number should replace the
question mark?

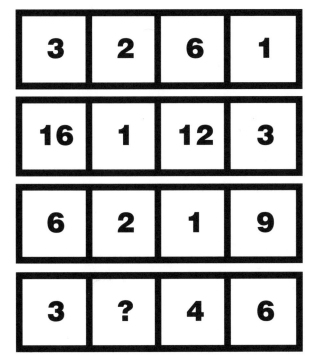

PUZZLE • 13 •

Which two words are closest in meaning?

Recent

Latent

Pleasing

Lurking

Manifest

Flanking

PUZZLE • 14 •

Which number should replace the
question mark?

PUZZLE • 15 •

Which set of numbers below has the same
relationship as **4-25-151** ?

A | **5 - 31 - 156**

B | **8 - 50 - 301**

C | **2 - 12 - 74**

D | **7 - 43 - 259**

• 16 •
PUZZLE

A man is lying in bed in his hotel room unable to get to sleep. He makes a telephone call to an adjoining room, says nothing, then puts down the telephone and goes to sleep. How come?

• 17 •
PUZZLE

Which number is the odd one out?

13   72   14   68   76   96   56   24   52   17   19

• 18 •
PUZZLE

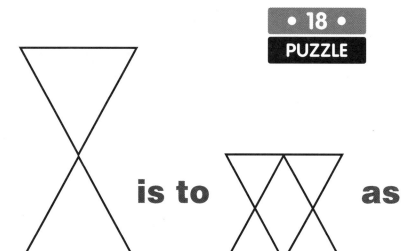 **is to** 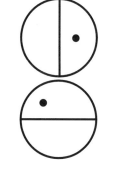 **as** **is to**

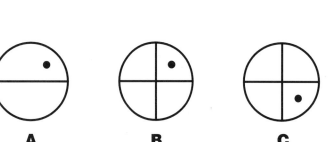

A   B   C   D   E

What letter should replace the
question mark?

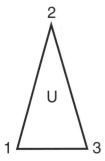

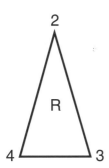

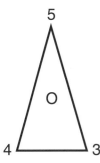

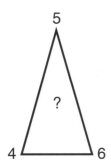

What number should replace the
question mark?

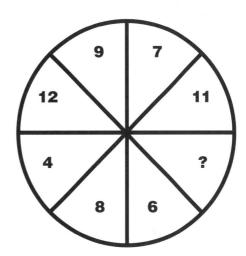

What is the meaning of Tamagotchi?

A. Japanese day

B. Fish

C. Bandit

D. Electronic toy

E. Members of a cult

What would you always find in a Grapnel?

A. Juice

B. Chocolate

C. Grapes

D. Claws

E. Music

S
E
C
T
I
O
N

4

• 23 •
PUZZLE

Tina has a large collection of pets. 1/3 of them are cats, 1/4 of them are dogs, 1/5 are hamsters and the rest are goldfish. If Tina has 39 goldfish, how many pets in total does she have?

• 24 •
PUZZLE

Which of the following circles should replace the question mark?

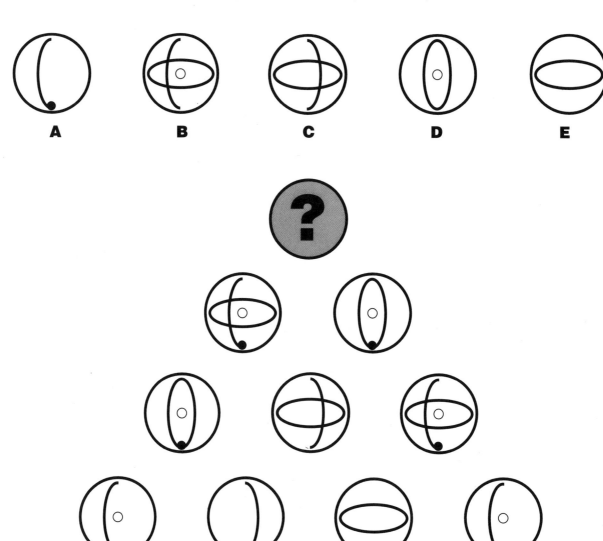

A   B   C   D   E

Which circle is nearest in content to A?

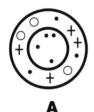

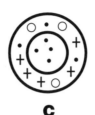
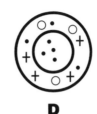

A   **B**   **C**   **D**   **E**

If yesterday's tomorrow was Thursday, what day falls on the day after tomorrow's yesterday?

Which number replaces the question mark?

 =10

 **=18**

 **=30**

 **=8**

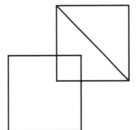 **=?**

• 28 •
PUZZLE

What number should replace the question mark?

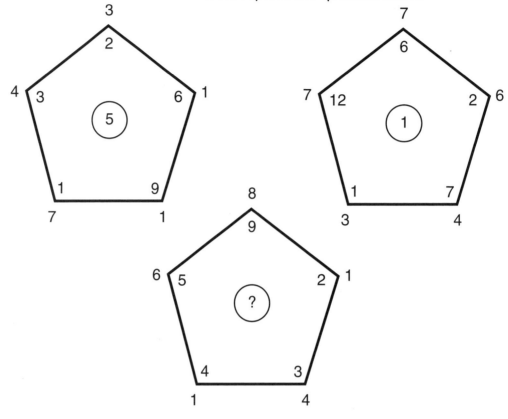

• 29 •
PUZZLE

Which two words mean the same?

Umbrage

Promise

Arbitrator

Offence

Unctuous

Corrupt

Invalidate

• 30 •
PUZZLE

If **Scrum Half** is to **Rugby**

Then **Silly Mid Off** is to

A. Netball

B. Hockey

C. Cricket

D. Soccer

E. Ice Hockey

• 1 •
PUZZLE

Which four of the five pieces below will fit together to form a perfect square?

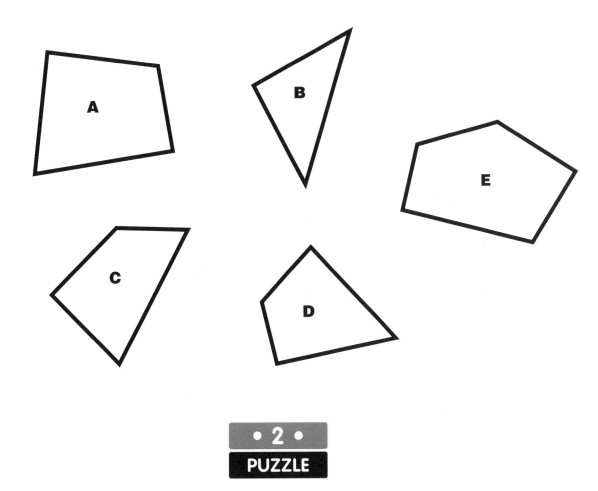

• 2 •
PUZZLE

Which two words are most similar in meaning?

Relate Advise Write Know Deceive Impart

• 3 •
PUZZLE

Which number should replace the question mark?

37	52	93	75	?

PUZZLE

One letter in the right-hand circle should be in the left-hand circle and vice versa. Can you find the two letters which need to be switched round?

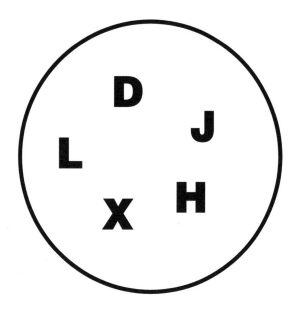

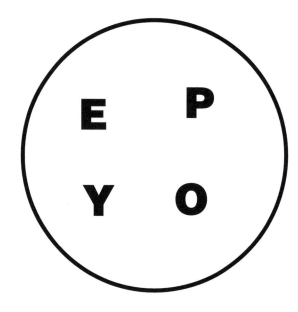

PUZZLE

Hint is to **Intimate** as **Proclaim** is to:

Divulge

Explain

Reveal

Promulgate

Announce

• 6 •
PUZZLE

Which geometric figure is described below?

"The intersection of line segments AB, BC and AC"

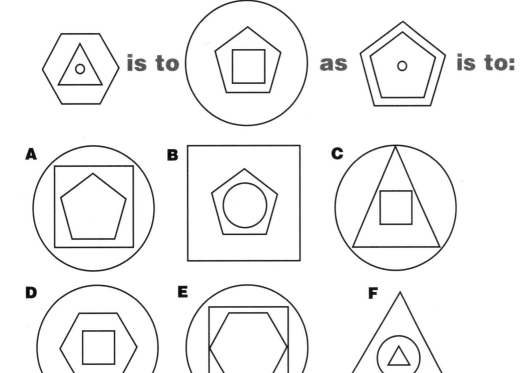

is to ... as ... is to:

A   B   C

D   E   F

Which set of figures is the odd one out?

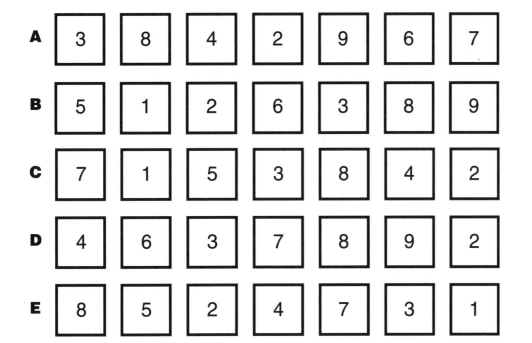

A	3	8	4	2	9	6	7
B	5	1	2	6	3	8	9
C	7	1	5	3	8	4	2
D	4	6	3	7	8	9	2
E	8	5	2	4	7	3	1

• 9 •
PUZZLE

Which word in brackets means the same as the word in capitals?

DESIRE
(Enthusiasm, Glean, Flatter, Expect, Covet)

• 10 •
PUZZLE

If a car had increased its average speed for a 210-mile journey by 5mph, the journey would have been completed in one hour less. What was the original speed of the car for the journey?

• 11 •
PUZZLE

Which is the missing tile?

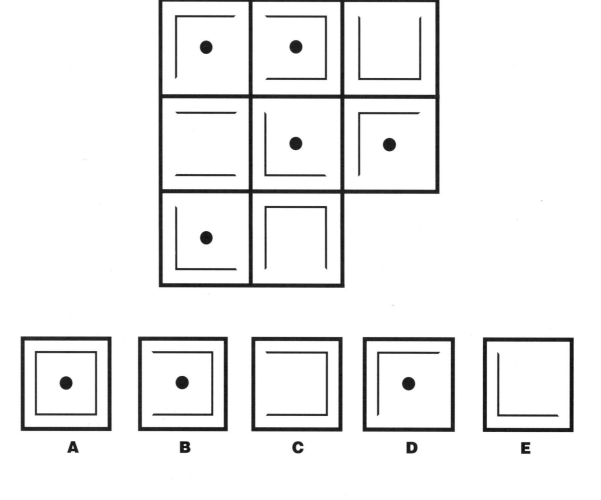

A   B   C   D   E

• 12 •
PUZZLE

Which clock face is the odd one out?

• 13 •
PUZZLE

What should appear at the bottom of the pyramid?

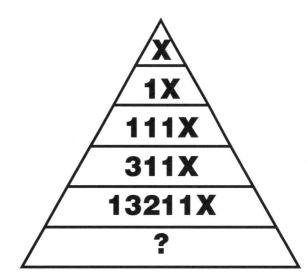

• 14 •
PUZZLE

Which is the odd one out?

Square

Equilateral

Pentagon

Hexagon

Rectangle

• 15 •
PUZZLE

Which letter is two below the letter immediately to the right of the letter immediately above the letter which comes three to the left of the letter N?

A	B	C	D	E	
F	G	H	I	J	
K	L	M	N	O	
P	Q	R	S	T	
U	V	W	X	Y	Z

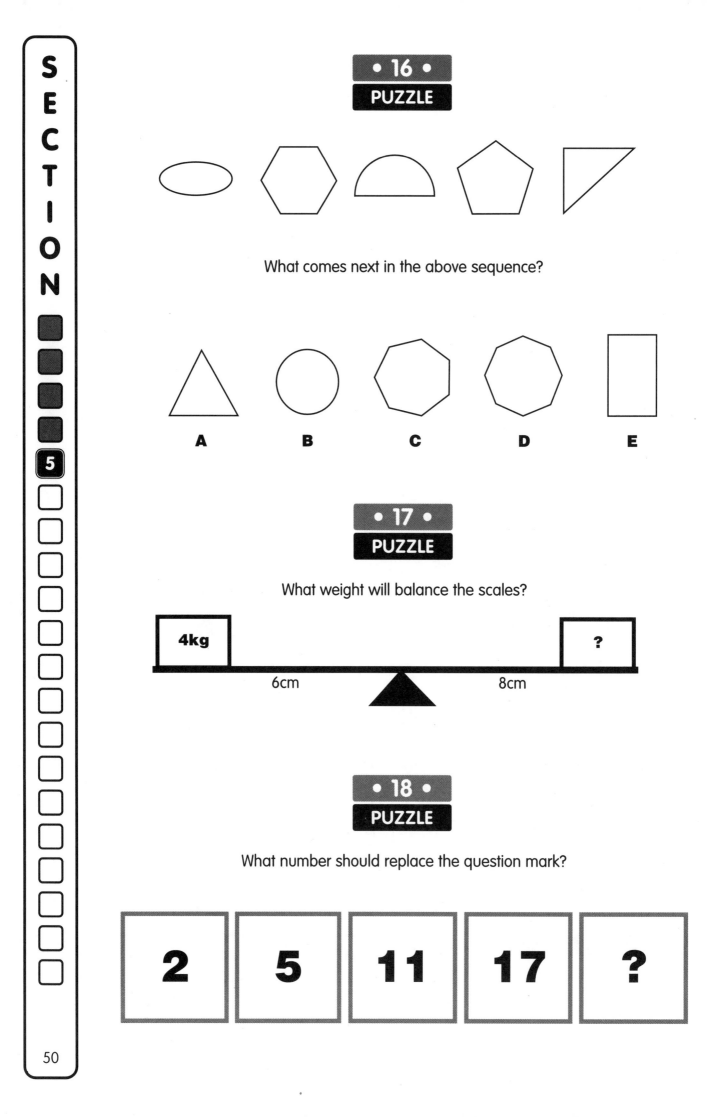

• 16 •
PUZZLE

What comes next in the above sequence?

A   B   C   D   E

• 17 •
PUZZLE

What weight will balance the scales?

4kg   ?

6cm   8cm

• 18 •
PUZZLE

What number should replace the question mark?

| 2 | 5 | 11 | 17 | ? |

Which two words are closest in meaning?

Infernal Malicious Rude Demonic

Parasitic Deranged

• 20 •
PUZZLE

How many circles appear below?

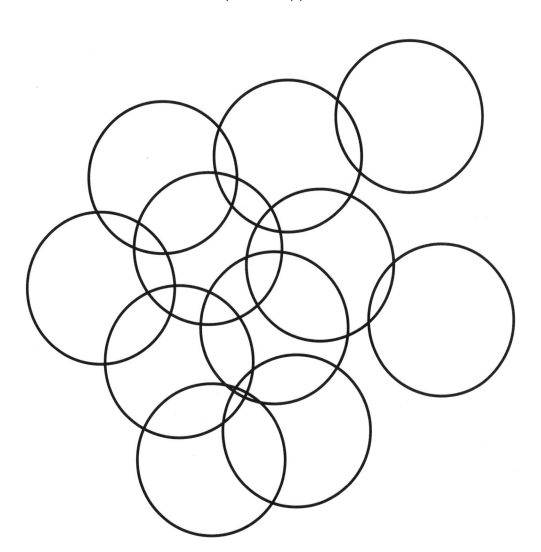

• 21 •
PUZZLE

What number should replace the question mark?

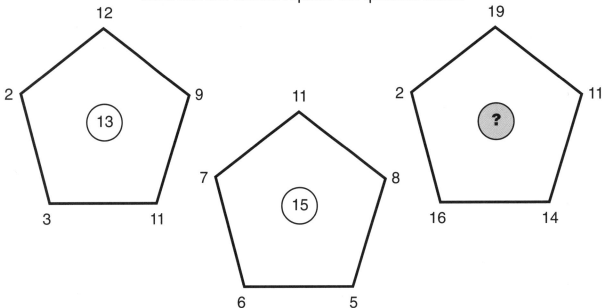

12
2   9
(13)
3   11

11
7   8
(15)
6   5

19
2   11
(?)
16   14

• 22 •
PUZZLE

A ball is dropped to the ground from a height of 10 ft. It then bounces up to half its original height then falls back. It repeats this always bouncing up half of the previous height. If the ball bounces on infinite number of times before coming to rest, how far in total does the ball travel?

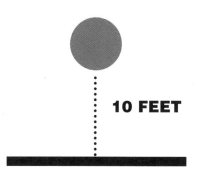

10 FEET

• 23 •
PUZZLE

Which number should replace the question mark?

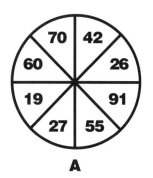

70	42
60	26
19	91
27	55

A

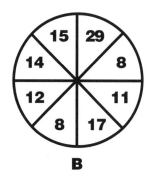

15	29
14	8
12	11
8	17

B

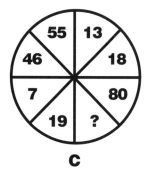

55	13
46	18
7	80
19	?

C

A day's production of motors has a 5% failure rate when tested. If 3 motors are tested at random what are the chances that all 3 would fail the test?

What number should replace the question mark?

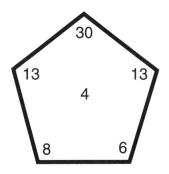 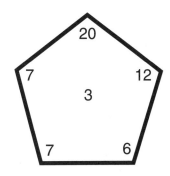 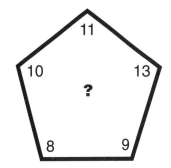

Complete this sequence.

3.5, 4, 7, 14, 49, ?

Find the answers to these 3 clues.

1	Like a fox	_ U _ P _ N _
2	A vegetable	_ U _ P _ I _
3	High priest	_ O _ T _ F _

S
E
C
T
I
O
N

5

• 28 •
PUZZLE

What would you always find in an Echeveria?

A. A horn

B. Brandy

C. A leaf

D. Sugar

E. Brimstone

• 29 •
PUZZLE

Which pair of letters replace the question marks?

POOR = FD

RICH = CH

NOW = EB

THEN = ??

• 30 •
PUZZLE

What number should replace the question mark?

6		48
	40	
5		25

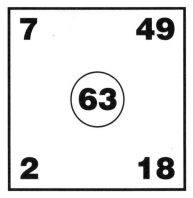

7		49
	63	
2		18

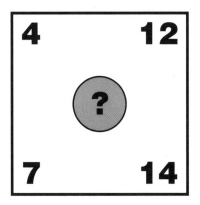

4		12
	?	
7		14

Divide the square into four identically shaped segments so that each segment contains one each of the four different symbols.

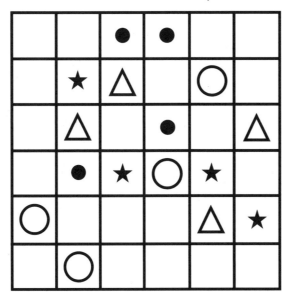

What is the difference between the average of the eight numbers below and the second highest odd number?

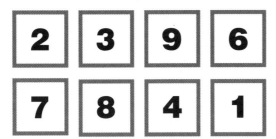

Which two words are closest in meaning?

Strong Elastic Stiff Limp Long Supple

• 4 •
PUZZLE

What letter should replace the question mark?

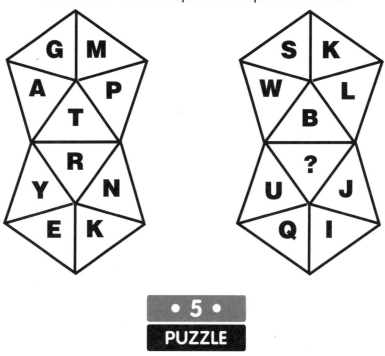

• 5 •
PUZZLE

Which is the odd one out?

Callow Venerable Unfledged Juvenile Adolescent

• 6 •
PUZZLE

What number should replace the question mark?

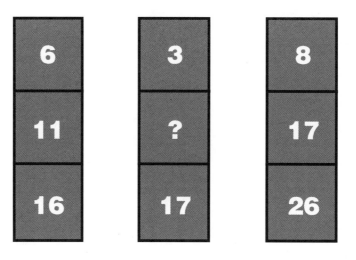

· 7 ·
PUZZLE

The houses are numbered 1, 2, 3, 4 etc. up one side of the street, then back down the other side. Opposite number 23 is number 48. How many houses are there in the street?

· 8 ·
PUZZLE

Which pair of letters is the odd one out?

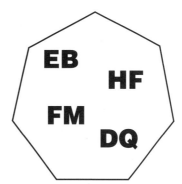

EB

HF

FM

DQ

· 9 ·
PUZZLE

Which letter completes the sequence?

A D F I J K N Q S ?

· 10 ·
PUZZLE

Which is the odd one out?

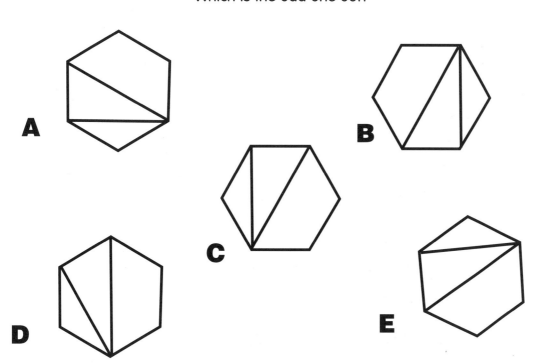

A

B

C

D

E

PUZZLE 11

What number should replace the question mark?

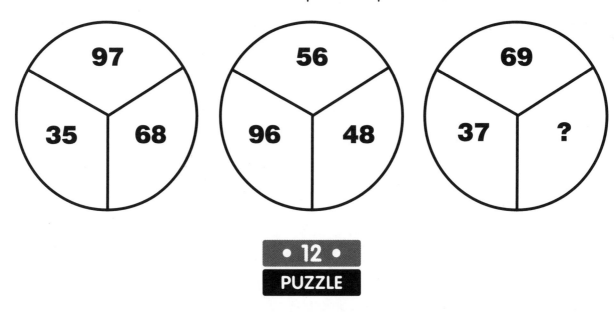

97

35 68

56

96 48

69

37 ?

PUZZLE 12

What letters should replace the question marks?

HJ   KN   OS   ??

PUZZLE 13

What number should replace the question mark?

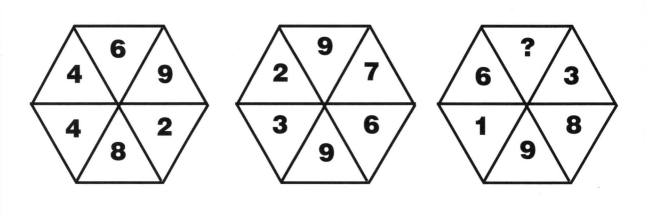

6
4   9
4   2
8

9
2   7
3   6
9

?
6   3
1   8
9

Which word in brackets is opposite in meaning to the word in capitals?

PIQUANT (Slow, Tart, Pleased, Bland, Irreverent)

What comes next **A, B, C, D,** or **E** in the sequence below?

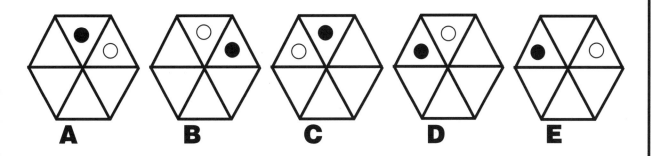

A   **B**   **C**   **D**   **E**

Divide 125 by 1/5, then add 5 and take away 10.

What is the answer?

PUZZLE • 17 •

What number should replace the question mark?

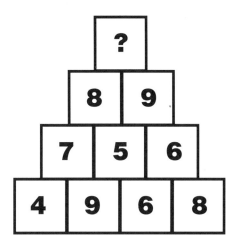

PUZZLE • 18 •

What letter should replace the question mark?

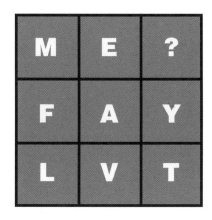

PUZZLE • 19 •

What number should replace the question mark?

1	4	14	45	139	?

PUZZLE • 20 •

A boy says, "I have as many brothers as sisters". His sister says, "I have twice as many brothers as sisters".

How many brothers and sisters are there in the family?

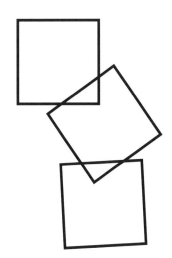
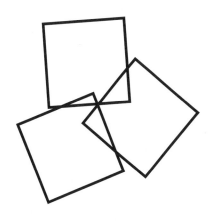
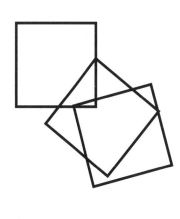

What continues the sequence occuring above?

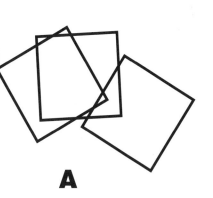

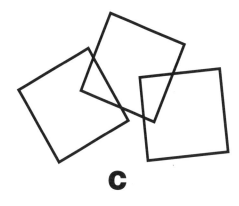

A

B

C

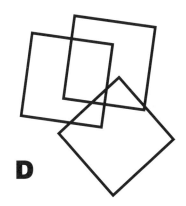
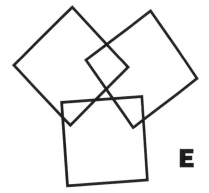

D

E

• 22 •
PUZZLE

Three tramps met in the woods. One had 3 loaves of bread, one had 2 loaves of bread, one had no loaves of bread but had $1. The loaves were shared equally.
How much did the third tramp pay to the other two?

S
E
C
T
I
O
N

6

• 23 •
PUZZLE

What number should replace the question mark?

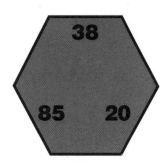
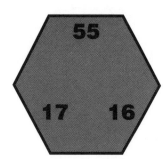

• 24 •
PUZZLE

What number should replace the question mark?

     ?

• 25 •
PUZZLE

How many squares are there in this diagram?

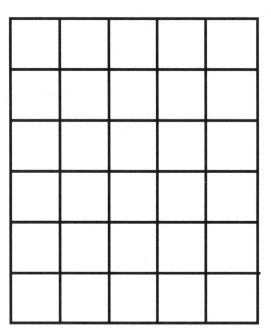

• 26 •
PUZZLE

Simplify:

$$\frac{19}{53} \div \frac{57}{106} = X$$

• 27 • PUZZLE

What is the meaning of Empyreal?

**A. Gratitude B. Loyalty
C. Heavenly D. Dismal
E. Patriotic**

• 28 • PUZZLE

What is always the colour of Incarnadine?

**A. Black
B. Green C. Blue
D. Yellow E. Red**

• 29 • PUZZLE

What is the name given to a group of Colts?

A. Rush B. Hover C. Horde D. Cluster E. Rag

• 30 • PUZZLE

What number should replace the question mark?

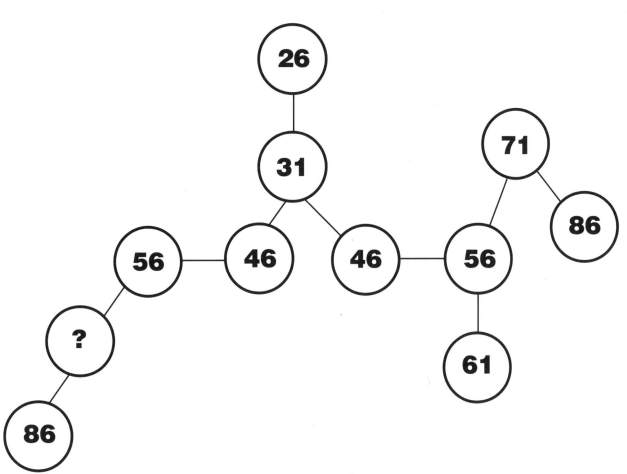

26
31
71
56 46 46 56 86
? 61
86

Which is the odd one out?

A

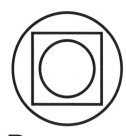

B

C

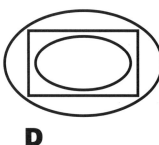

D

E

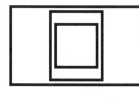

F

Which letters should replace the question marks?

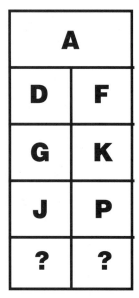

Which two words are closest in meaning?

Overt

Eventual

Ulterior

Basic

Covert

Motive

• 4 •
PUZZLE

What number should replace the question mark?

9 3
4 2
5 7
10

6 1
6 7
2 5
9

5 1
6 4
2 3
?

• 5 •
PUZZLE

What number should replace the question mark?

3	2	7
8	4	?
1	6	5

• 6 •
PUZZLE

What continues the above sequence?

 **A**   **B**  **C**

 **D**  **E**

65

PUZZLE

A man jogs at 6mph over a certain distance and walks back very slowly over the same route at 2mph. What is his average speed for the journey?

PUZZLE

What number should replace the question mark?

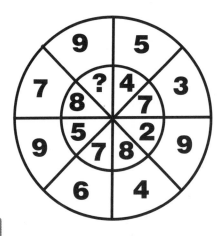

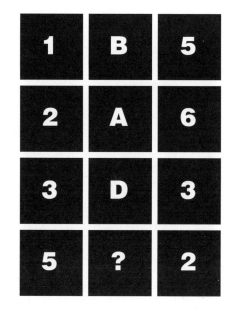
PUZZLE

Turret is to Watchtower as Barbican is to:

Gatehouse

Courtyard

Wall

Mound

Drawbridge

PUZZLE

What letter should replace the question mark?

• 11 •
PUZZLE

What comes next in the sequence?

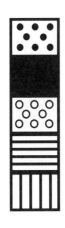  

A   **B**   **C**   **D**   **E**

• 12 •
PUZZLE

Each symbol in this table has a value. The total of these values in each row and column is written at the end of the corresponding row or column.
Can you find the value of each symbol?

20.7	△	□	△	△
29.7	□	□	□	◇
38.2	△	◇	○	○
32.6	□	◇	○	△
	23.4	**30.6**	**37.3**	**29.9**

• 13 •
PUZZLE

What number should complete the bottom line?

2	3	1
4	2	4
7	6	4
6	8	10
16	17	15
23	21	23
40	39	?

S
E
C
T
I
O
N

7

67

What is Litany?

A. Grace
B. Prayer
C. Figure of speech
D. Writ
E. Uniform

What number is missing?

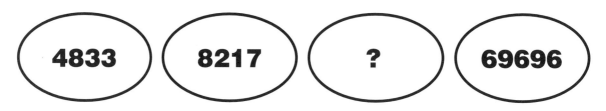

4833   8217   ?   69696

What number should replace the question mark?

147   159   174   186   ?

PUZZLE 17

What number is missing?

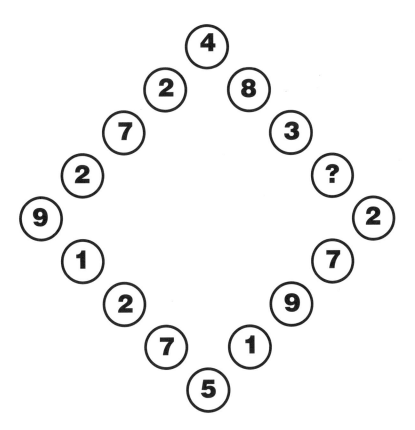

PUZZLE 18

Which two words are opposite in meaning?

Wistful
Loved
Wrathful
Strained
Mindful
Contented

• 19 •
PUZZLE

Which letter is immediately to the right of the letter two places to the right of the letter immediately to left of the letter two places to the right of the letter B?

• 20 •
PUZZLE

Which is the odd one out?

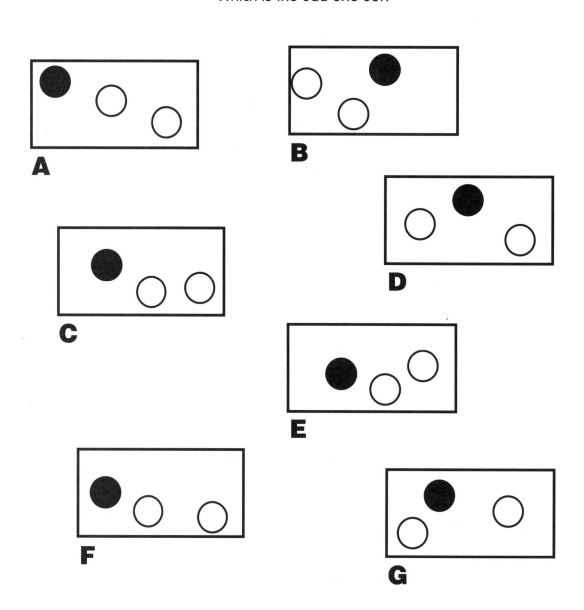

• 21 •
PUZZLE

What number should replace the question mark?

| 1 | 11 | 21 | 1211 | 111221 | ? |

• 22 •
PUZZLE

What number should replace the question mark?

10   54   11¼   42¾   12½   31½   **?**

• 23
PUZZLE

Multiply the largest even number by the smallest odd number.

81	14	28
18	87	83
91	22	44

• 24 •
PUZZLE

Simplify:

$$\frac{6}{17} \div \frac{36}{51} = X$$

PUZZLE

What is the meaning of Heliocentric?

A. Starry
B. Spiralled
C. Signalled
D. Dead centre
E. Sun centred

PUZZLE

Which number replaces the question mark to complete the sequence?

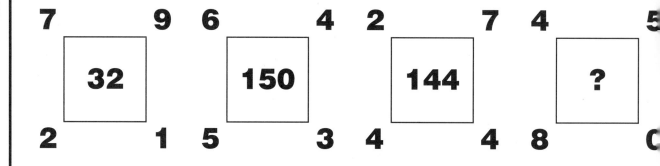

PUZZLE

Which two words are the same?

Raillery Joviality Aptness
Impatience Banter Kindness

• 28 •
PUZZLE

A man is in pitch dark-ness, he only has four socks in his drawer – a mixture of black and white. The chances of drawing out a white pair is 1/2.

What are the chances of drawing out a black pair?

• 29 •
PUZZLE

There is a 5-digit number which is three times as large with a "1" after it as it is with a "1" before it.

What is it?

• 30 •
PUZZLE

What historical event does this portray?

PUZZLE

Which is the odd one out?

Raven Jet Sable Hazel Ebony

• 2 •
PUZZLE

What number should replace the question mark?

• 3 •
PUZZLE

A company offers a wage increase to its workforce, providing it increases production by 2.4% per week. If the company works a 6-day week, by how much per day must the workforce increase production to achieve the desired target?

PUZZLE

What number should replace the question mark?

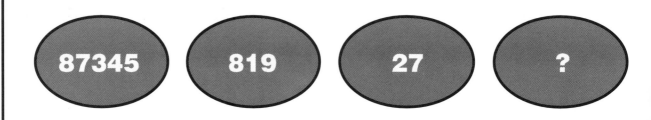

87345   819   27   ?

PUZZLE 5

What comes next in this sequence?

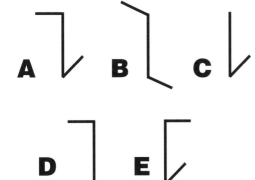

A B C

D E

PUZZLE 6

Almanac is to **Inform** as **Baedeker** is to:

Pray
Teach
Guide
Text
Instruct

PUZZLE 7

What letter should replace the question mark?

PUZZLE 8

What number should replace the question mark?

2	9	7	3	3
7	8	4	7	4
5	2	2	8	3
1	2	3	8	6
9	9	1	2	?

SECTION

8

75

PUZZLE 9

Which two words are closest in meaning?

Doubtful
Hypothetical
Untrue
Assumed
Actual
Narcotic

PUZZLE 10

What number should replace the question mark?

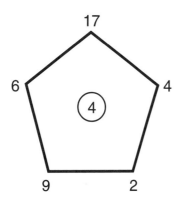
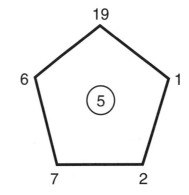
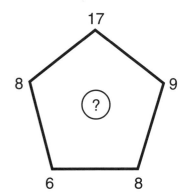

17
6   4
(4)
9   2

19
6   1
(5)
7   2

17
8   9
(?)
6   8

• 11 •
PUZZLE

What letter should replace the question mark?

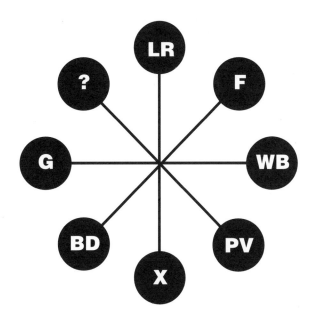

• 12 •
PUZZLE

Sally has half as many again as Jenny who has half as many again as Tony.
Altogether they have 361.
How many has Jenny?

• 13 •
PUZZLE

What number should replace the question mark?

3 12 15 60 63 ?

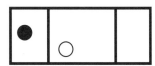
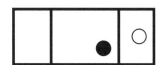
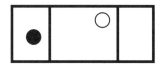

Which option below continues the above sequence?

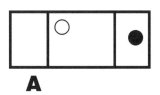
A

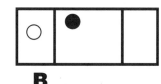
B

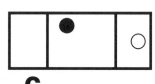
C

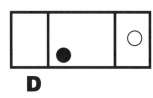
D

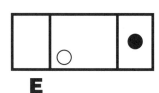
E

• 15 •
PUZZLE

Which letter should replace the question mark?

A	Y	C
U	E	W
G	?	I

• 16 •
PUZZLE

What number should replace the question mark?

3	7	18	42
12	5	9	60
9	8	4	32
6	3	7	?

• 17 •
PUZZLE

What figure is defined below?

"A set of all points in a plane at a fixed distance from a fixed point in the plane".

• 18 •
PUZZLE

What symbol should replace the question mark?

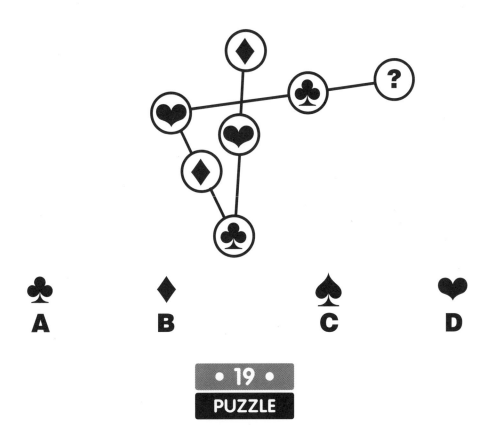

A B C D

• 19 •
PUZZLE

What number should replace the question mark?

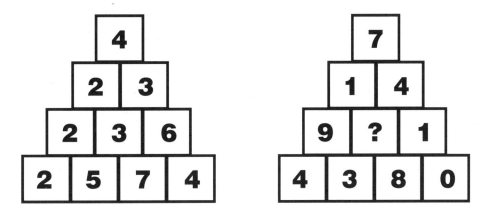

• 20 •
PUZZLE

What letter should replace the question mark?

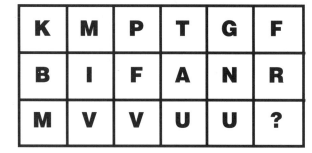

K	M	P	T	G	F
B	I	F	A	N	R
M	V	V	U	U	?

• 21 •
PUZZLE

Simplify:

-6 x 4 - 3 x 6 + 17 = x

• 22 •
PUZZLE

What number should replace the question mark?

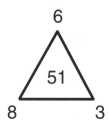 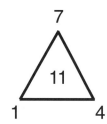 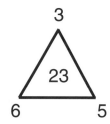 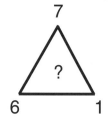

6 / 51 / 8 3

7 / 11 / 1 4

3 / 23 / 6 5

7 / ? / 6 1

• 23 •
PUZZLE

Which number should replace the question mark?

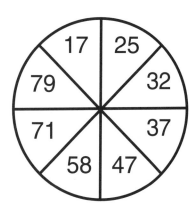 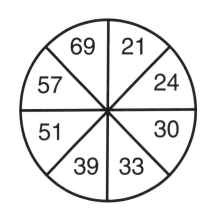 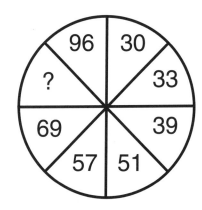

SECTION

8

• 24 •
PUZZLE

Which letters replace the question marks to complete the puzzle?

• 25 •
PUZZLE

Complete this obscure puzzle to form a logical seqence.

8 4 7 6

2 4 1 7 ?

• 26 •
PUZZLE

What is Ecarte?

A. A flag B. A battle cry C. Brandy D. Soup E. A card game

• 27 •
PUZZLE

Which two words are opposite to each other?

A. Educe
B. Efficient
C. Emanation
D. Intuit
E. Effluence
F. Manifesto

Find the missing number.

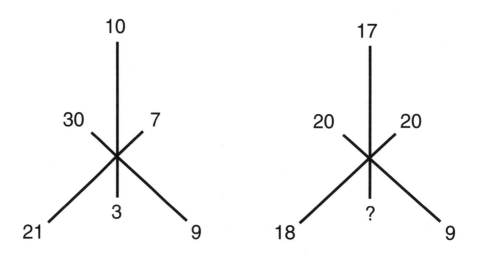

A farmer has 200 yards of fencing and he wishes to enclose an area of the greatest possible size. What is the area of the largest piece of land he can enclose with his fencing?

Which of these cubes cannot be formed from this web?

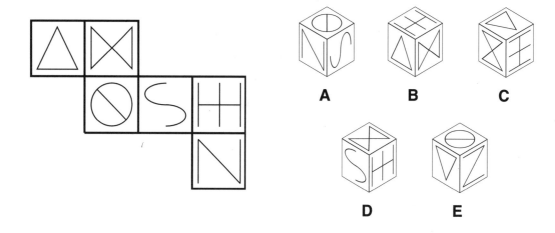

PUZZLE • 1 •

The bag of potatoes weighed three-quarters of its weight plus 2¼lbs.
How much did the bag of potatoes weigh?

PUZZLE • 2 •

Which number should replace the question mark?

7	4	8	6
2	7	1	5
5	6	6	8
6	3	5	?

PUZZLE • 3 •

What letters should replace the question marks?

D	G	H	C	H	E
F	E	?	?	G	D
H	A	H	F	B	?
C	F	E	H	G	F
?	G	B	F	C	G
H	D	G	D	G	E

PUZZLE 4

Which is the odd one out?

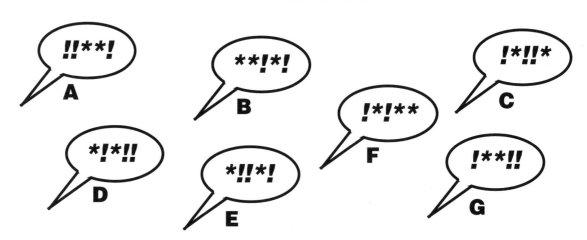

A: !!**!
B: **!*!
C: !*!!*
D: *!*!!
E: *!!*!
F: !*!**
G: !**!!

PUZZLE 5

Which two words are opposite in meaning?

Smooth   Evasive   Shameful   Noisy   Candid   Shunned

PUZZLE 6

What number should replace the question mark?

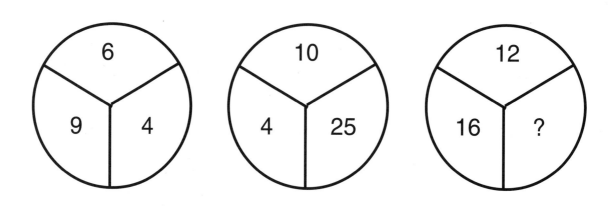

6   9   4

10   4   25

12   16   ?

• 7 •
PUZZLE

How many times can the word 'PATH' be read? Start at the central letter 'P' and move to an adjoining letter up, down, backward or forward, in and out in any direction.

• 8 •
PUZZLE

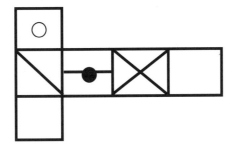

When the above is folded to form a cube, just one of the following can be produced. Which one?

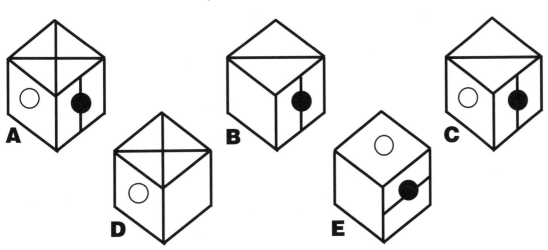

A   B   C   D   E

• 9 •
PUZZLE

Each symbol in this table has a value. The total of these values in each row and column is written at the end of the corresponding row or column.
Can you find the value of each symbol?

21.4	△	□	△	□
26.3	△	○	□	□
30.2	◇	○	△	△
28.8	◇	◇	○	◇
	24.6	32.8	28.6	20.7

• 10 •
PUZZLE

Work from top left to top right by moving from square to square horizontally and vertically to unravel a logical sequence. Diagonal moves are not permitted and every square must be used only once.

A	B	V	W
E	D	T	S
G	K	M	Q
H	J	N	P

• 11 •
PUZZLE

A car travels 80 miles in the time that another car travelling 10mph faster travels 100 miles.
What is the speed of the faster car?

• 12 •
PUZZLE

What number should replace the question mark?

384	288	144	36	27	?

PUZZLE • 13 •

What numbers should replace the question marks?

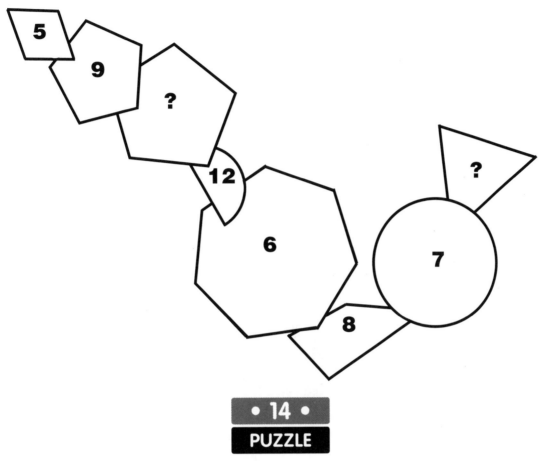

PUZZLE • 14 •

Which letter should replace the question mark?

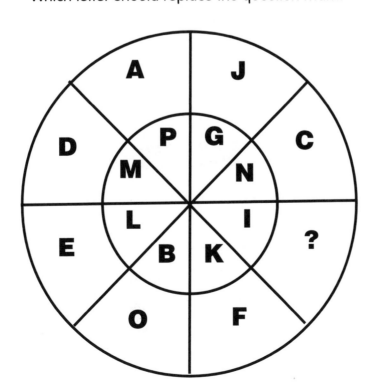

• 15 • PUZZLE

Cravat is to **Neck** as **Kepi** is to:

**Shoulders
Legs
Feet
Head
Arms**

• 16 • PUZZLE

What time should be shown on the fifth clock face?

18:56   19:16

19:33

19:49   ?

• 17 • PUZZLE

What number should replace the question mark?

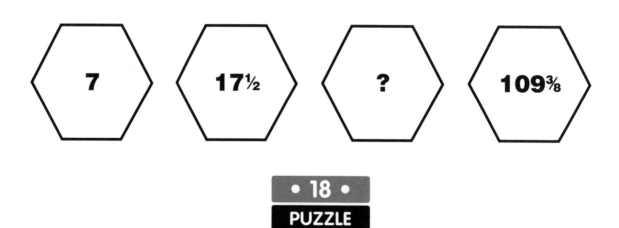

7   17½   ?   109⅜

• 18 • PUZZLE

Which letter should replace the question mark?

A	Z
C	R

C	W
G	M

E	T
K	?

What number should replace the question
mark?

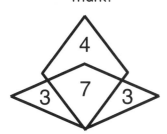

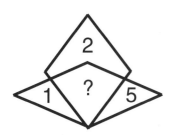

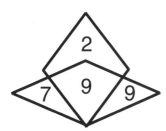

SUNDAY
MONDAY
TUESDAY
WEDNESDAY
THURSDAY
FRIDAY
SATURDAY

What day comes immediately before the
day that is two days after the day
immediately after the day which comes
two days before the day which comes
three days after Tuesday?

What number should replace the question mark?

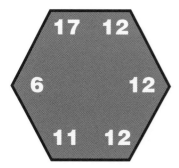

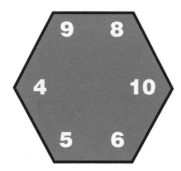

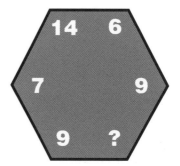

• 22 •
PUZZLE

If 8 x 9 = 200
7 x 7 = ?

• 23 •
PUZZLE

A linking of contradictory terms is called an oxymoron, for example, bitter sweet. Find 6 oxymorons below.

**Holiday Never Ugly
Miracle Strangely Familiar
Working Death Again
Minor Living Pretty**

• 24 •
PUZZLE

Which six-letter word can be made from these four letters?

Y	U
L	F

25
PUZZLE

What did Elmer A. Sperry invent?

A. A glider
B. A microscope
C. A dishwasher
D. A crossword puzzle
E. A gyro-compass

26
PUZZLE

What phrase is indicated below?

POOH

MUM

27
PUZZLE

Six playing cards are lying face down. Two of them are kings. You pick 2 cards at random.
What is the more likely?

A. There will be at least one king
B. There will be no king.

SECTION

9

• 28 •
PUZZLE

How many revolutions are made by a 26" bicycle wheel over one mile?

• 29 •
PUZZLE

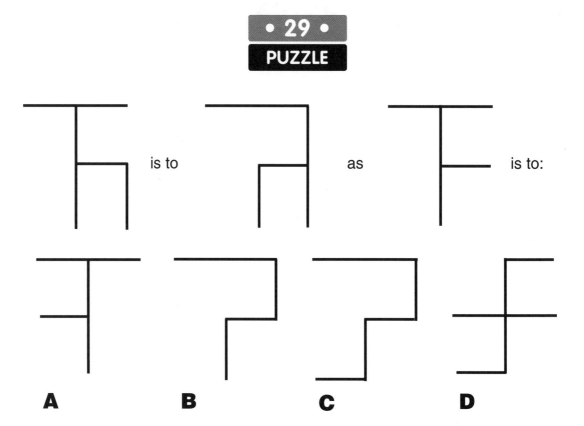

is to   as   is to:

A   **B**   **C**   **D**

• 30 •
PUZZLE

What is the name given to a group of Turkeys?

A. Husk
B. Rafter
C. Clutch
D. Hunt
E. Rayful

• 1 •
PUZZLE

How many triangles appear below?

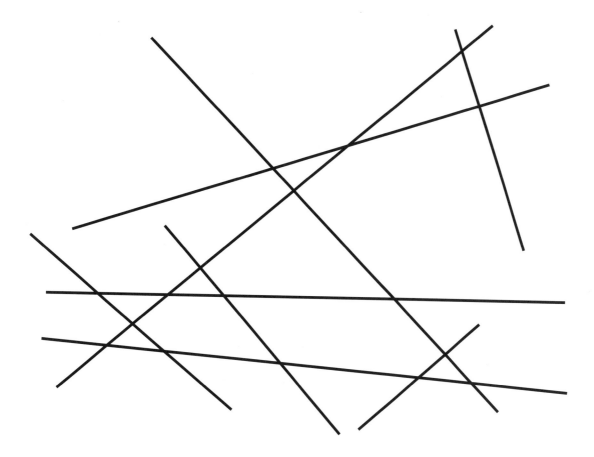

• 2 •
PUZZLE

Which is the odd one out?

**Shrivel
Sully
Wizen
Wither
Shrink**

• 3 •
PUZZLE

What number comes next?

4217
9313
7452
1829
?

**A. 3941 B. 4972 C. 6616
D. 5479 E. 3274**

**S
E
C
T
I
O
N**

10

PUZZLE • 4 •

Which number is the odd one out?

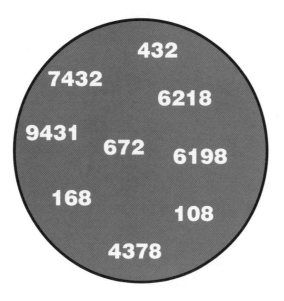

PUZZLE • 5 •

The letters AFGMZP appear in a logical
pattern in the grid below.
Which two
letters are in the wrong position?

A	F	G	M	Z	P	A
P	Z	M	G	F	A	P
Z	P	A	F	G	M	Z
M	F	G	A	P	Z	M
G	M	Z	P	A	F	G
F	A	P	Z	M	G	F
A	F	G	M	Z	P	A

PUZZLE • 6 •

Which word in brackets is opposite to the word in capitals?

PROSCRIBE (Curtail, Interdict, Allow, Betray, Extend)

PUZZLE • 7 •

One of these sequences represents a chemical compound, and the other represents
a building block of matter. Can you work out what they are?

A B C D E F G H I J K L M

H I J K L M N O

• 8 •
PUZZLE

At the end of the meeting the 14 people present all shake hands with each other once. How many handshakes is that altogether?

• 9 •
PUZZLE

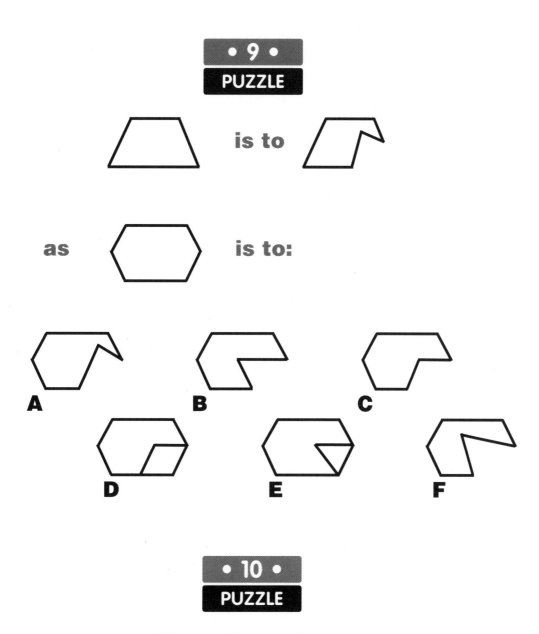

is to

as

is to:

A   B   C

D   E   F

• 10 •
PUZZLE

Sapphire is to **Blue** as **Melanite** is to:

Yellow
Black
Brown
White
Red

What number should replace the question mark?

1
0
4
1

2
3
2

3
5

?

Which letter should replace the question mark?

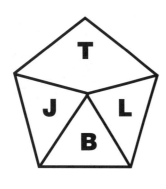

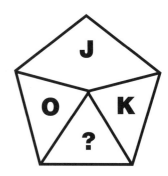

• 13 •
PUZZLE

A batsman is out for 10 runs which reduces his batting average for the season from 34 to 32. How many runs would he have needed to score to increase his average from 34 to 37?

Which number will satisfy the following condition?

"If you multiply the number by three, or add three to it, you get the same result."

PUZZLE • 15 •

What number should replace the question mark?

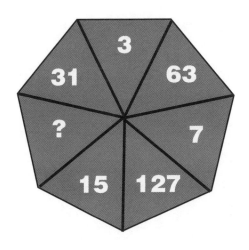

PUZZLE • 16 •

What letter should replace the question mark?

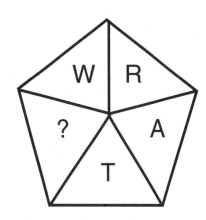

PUZZLE • 17 •

Which number should replace the question mark?

100   90   81   73   ?

PUZZLE • 18 •

How many minutes is it before 9am if 1½ hours ago it was twice as many minutes past 5am?

• 19 •
PUZZLE

What number should replace the question mark?

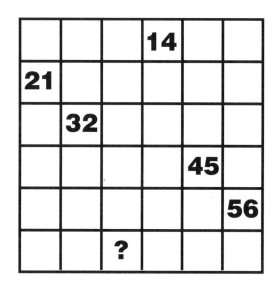

			14		
21					
	32				
				45	
					56
		?			

• 20 •
PUZZLE

What number should replace the question mark? Each letter represents a different value.

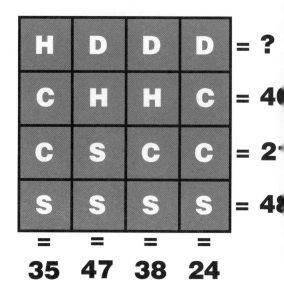

H	D	D	D	= ?
C	H	H	C	= 4●
C	S	C	C	= 2●
S	S	S	S	= 48
=	=	=	=	
35	47	38	24	

• 21 •
PUZZLE

Which letters should replace the question marks?

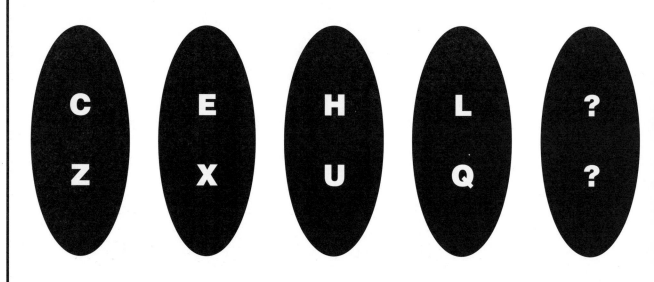

C
Z

E
X

H
U

L
Q

?
?

• 22 • PUZZLE

Simplify:

$$3 - 2 \times 6 + 4 \div 3 = x$$

• 23 • PUZZLE

What number should replace the question mark?

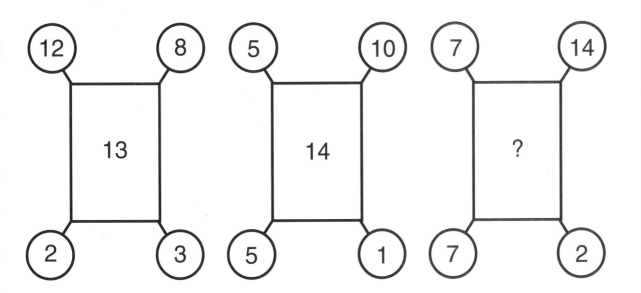

• 24 • PUZZLE

What number should replace the question mark?

• 25 •
PUZZLE

What is always part of Jeremiad?

A. Grief
B. Container
C. Wine
D. A hymn
E. A vehicle

• 26 •
PUZZLE

Which number replaces the question mark to complete the sequence?

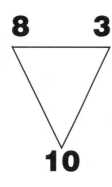 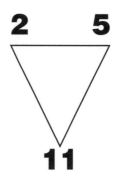 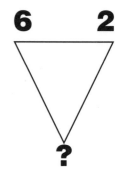

8   3   2   5   6   2

10   11   ?

• 27 •
PUZZLE

Which two words mean the same?

Background
Mien
Deceit
Bearing
Conflict
Inclination

• 28 •
PUZZLE

What number should replace the question mark?

7121   7110   7101   7092   ?

• 29 •
PUZZLE

What value weight should replace the question mark to balance the scale?

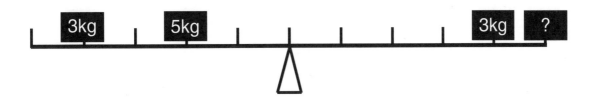

3kg   5kg   3kg   ?

• 30 •
PUZZLE

What is the opposite of Refractory?

A. Attribute
B. Obedient
C. Perverse
D. Unruly
E. Meditative

S
E
C
T
I
O
N

10

•1• PUZZLE

Which four of the five pieces below will fit together to form a perfect square?

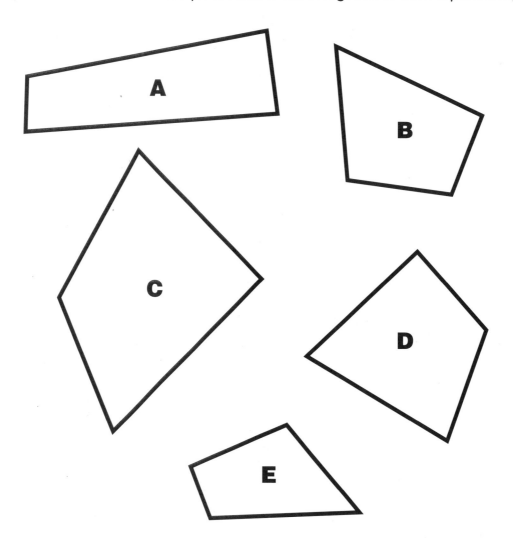

A

B

C

D

E

•2• PUZZLE

Which car number plate is the odd one out?

G343 CDC	F216 BAF
A	B

E215 BAE	H512 EAB
C	D

•3• PUZZLE

What numbers should replace the question marks?

3	6	10	13	?
4	6	9	15	?

• 4 • PUZZLE

Tachograph is to **Record** as **Pantograph** is to:

Copy Transmit Photograph Detect Maintain

• 5 • PUZZLE

Which number should replace the question mark?

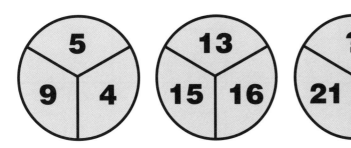

• 6 • PUZZLE

What comes next in this sequence?

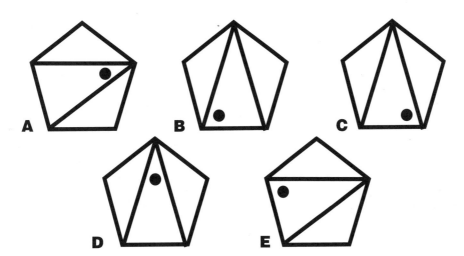

PUZZLE

Which two words are opposite in meaning?

Exiguous   Direct   Slow   Meandering   Doubtful   Liberal

PUZZLE

Which section is missing?

2	9	3	3
7	2		7
4	6		
4	0	8	5

0	A
4	3

1	B
5	2

2	C
5	3

3	D
2	2

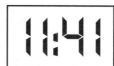

PUZZLE

**My house is ninth from one end of the row and fifteenth from the other end.
How many houses are there in the row?**

PUZZLE

What time is missing from the fifth clock face?

  11:41 12:03 ?

104

Which circle should replace the question mark?

A

B

C

D

E

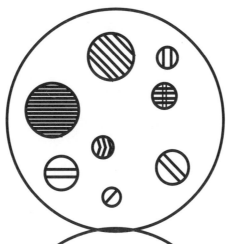

F

G

H

I

J

• 12 •
PUZZLE

Which is the odd one out?

Pier

Jetty

Quay

Port

Wharf

• 13 •
PUZZLE

What number is missing from the outer ring?

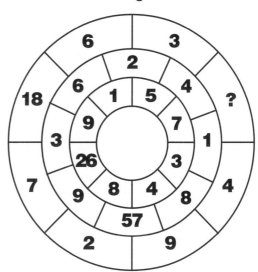

I purchased 12 items for $24. Some items were $1, some were $3 and some were $4. How many items at each of the prices did I purchase?

What letter should replace the question mark?

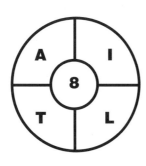

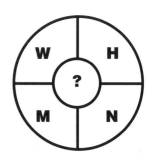

• 16 •
PUZZLE

What number should replace the question mark?

• 17 •
PUZZLE

What letter should replace the question mark?

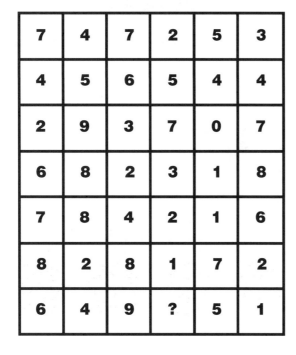

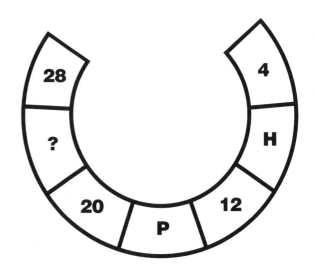

How many circles contain a dot?

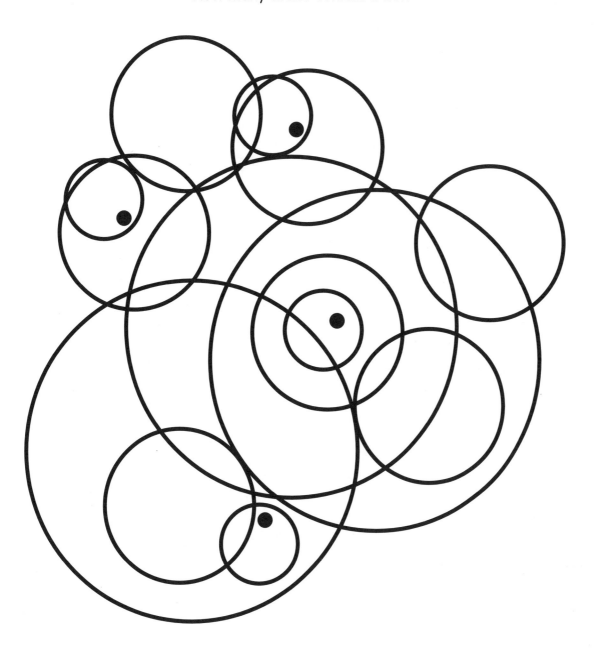

• 19 •
PUZZLE

What number should replace the question mark?

1 1 2 6 24 24 48 ?

• 20 • PUZZLE

What number should replace the question mark?

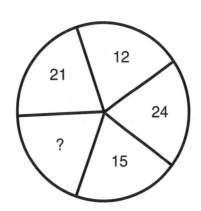

21 12
24
? 15

• 21 • PUZZLE

What replaces the question mark to complete the puzzle?

WHEN   HERE   IF

NOW   THEN   WHO

LAST   THERE   ?

• 22 • PUZZLE

Insert a word into each pair of brackets that will complete the first word and begin the second. (Dashes indicate the number of letters in each word.)

WEAT (_ _ _) MIT

DE (_ _ _ _) ROY

CONTR (_ _ _) ING

CR (_ _ _) ALE

ENT (_ _ _ _) LE

• 23 • PUZZLE

There are three non-standard dice to be used in a simple gambling game were the winner is the person with the highest roll. Each player may choose any one of the dice whose sides have the values shown below.

Which one, if any, would you pick to give you an advantage over the other players?

Dice A   3   4   8   3   4   8

Dice B   1   5   9   1   5   9

Dice C   2   6   7   2   6   7

• 24 • PUZZLE

After the card game, the 4 gamblers had $233 between them.

Don had $20 more than Henry

$53 more than Cecil

$71 more than Sid

How much did each have?

• 25 • PUZZLE

Which of these tetrahedra (regular, 4-sided triangular pyramids) can be formed from this web?

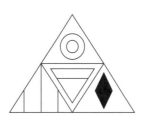

• 26 • PUZZLE

Which option completes the puzzle?

HOLY is to SLOB

As LOW is to ???

TON   WIT   OLD

SIN   PUT

• 27 • PUZZLE

If **Mathematics** is to **Rhomboid** then **Medicine** is to:

A. Spheroid

B. Trapezium

C. Parameter

D. Atropine

E. Ellipsoid

SECTION

11

109

PUZZLE

Which two words mean the opposite?

Memorial Ignominy Thraldom Dignity Liberty Strategem

• 29 •
PUZZLE

Which circle replaces the circle with the question mark? There is a logical sequence starting at the base.

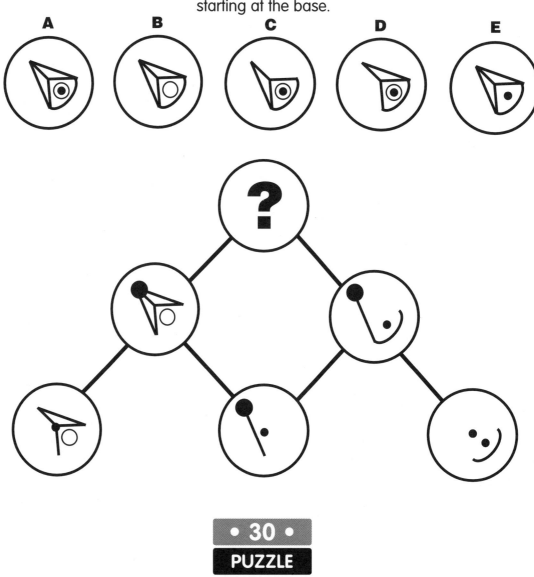

• 30 •
PUZZLE

Two golfers had a challenge match. One scored 69 and one scored 72. The player who scored 72 won, there were no handicaps. Why?

•1• PUZZLE

Which is the odd one out?

Joke Laugh Chortle Titter Snigger

•2• PUZZLE

Which of these diagrams is the odd one out?

A

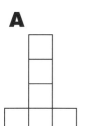

C

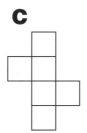

E

B

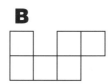

D

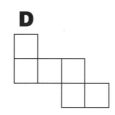

•3• PUZZLE

A	+	F	=	N
H	+	D	=	X
B	+	F	=	?

• 4 • PUZZLE

What comes next in the above sequence?

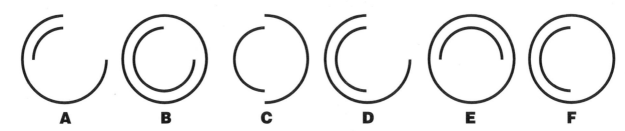

A   B   C   D   E   F

• 5 • PUZZLE

What letter or letters should replace the question mark?

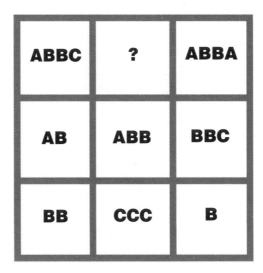

ABBC	?	ABBA
AB	ABB	BBC
BB	CCC	B

• 6 • PUZZLE

Which word in brackets means the same as the word in capitals?

EQUABLE
(Inquiring, Nervous, Fair, Placid, Alike)

PUZZLE

What option replaces the question mark to complete the sequence?

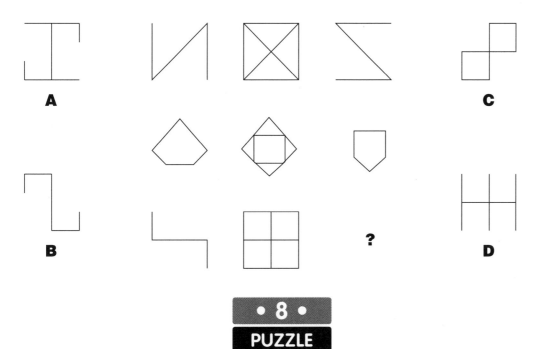

A

C

B

?

D

• 8 •

PUZZLE

How many circles appear below?

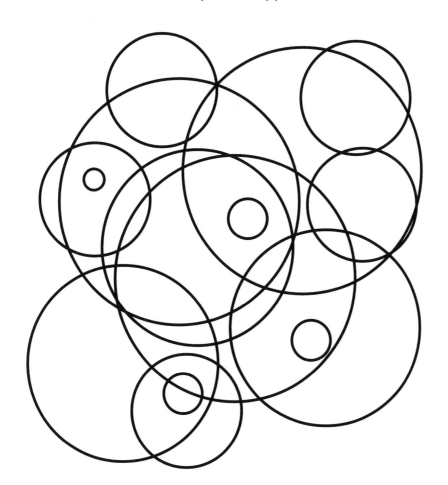

• 9 •
PUZZLE

What number should replace the question mark?

		7		
	9	2	1	
11	5	5	4	2
13 8	9	9	8	3 5
13	14	14	10	13
	20	17	21	
		?		

• 10 •
PUZZLE

Tommy dropped a sugar cube in his coffee, was called away to answer the telephone and, on his return 10 minutes later, lifted the sugar cube out of his coffee intact. How was he able to do this?

• 11 •
PUZZLE

Which number should replace the question mark?

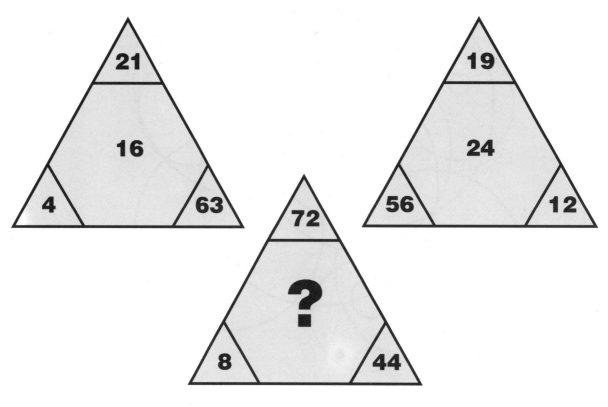

Triangle 1: 21, 16, 4, 63

Triangle 2: 19, 24, 56, 12

Triangle 3: 72, ?, 8, 44

• 12 •
PUZZLE

What comes next in this sequence?

1.000, 1.414, 1.732, 2.000, 2.236, 2.449, ?

• 13 •
PUZZLE

Which number should replace the question mark?

(4) (6) (8) (9) (10) (12) (14)

(15) (16) (18) (20) (21) (22) (?)

• 14 •
PUZZLE

The link between the numbers in each
line is the same.
Can you fill in the missing numbers?

| 78 | — | 312 | — | ? |

| 54 | — | ? | — | 72 |

| 24 | — | ? | — | ? |

• 15 •
PUZZLE

IF 5 X 4 = 32

THEN

5 X 5 = ?

• 16 • PUZZLE

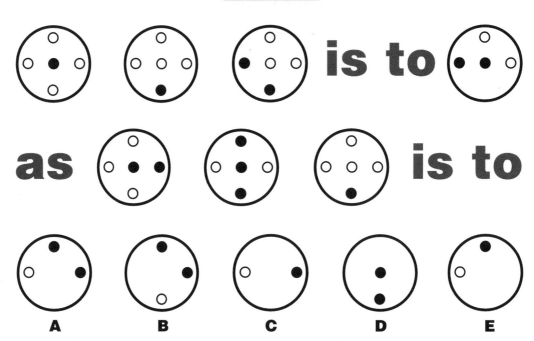

is to

as

is to

A   B   C   D   E

• 17 • PUZZLE

What number is 45

less than when it is

multiplied by six

times itself?

• 18 • PUZZLE

What number should replace the question mark?

3	8	11	19
4	5	9	14
7	13	20	33
11	18	29	?

• 19 • PUZZLE

Which letter is three to the left of the letter immediately to the right of the letter which comes midway between the letter two to the right of the letter B and two to the left of the letter H?

A	B	C	D	E	F	G	H

Which number replaces the question mark to complete the puzzle?

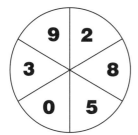 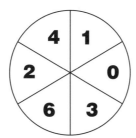 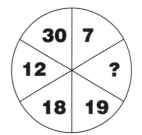

What is the value of x ?

$$\frac{7}{16} \div \frac{21}{32} = x$$

Simplify

$$7 - 16 \times 2 - 3 - 6 \times 4 = x$$

What number should replace the question mark?

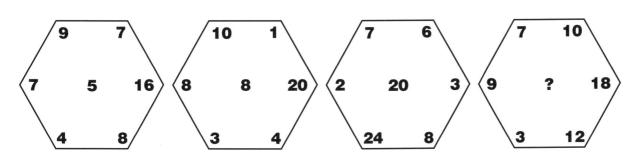

S E C T I O N

12

117

• 24 • PUZZLE

What is the angle between the lines BD and DF?

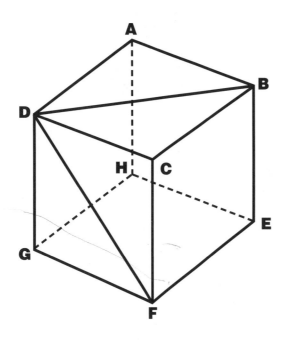

• 25 • PUZZLE

Each symbol in this table has a value. The total of these values in each row and column is written at the end of the corresponding row or column.
Can you find the value of each symbol?

	col1	col2	col3	col4
30.3	△	☐	☐	☐
3.7	△	☐	◇	◇
7.2	○	△	○	◇
15.6	○	△	○	○
	4.8	**14.6**	**22.9**	**14.5**

• 26 • PUZZLE

All numbers used in this question are written in modulo 9. Can you solve the sum?

4 5

+

1 4 8

= ?

• 27 • PUZZLE

Which number replaces the question mark to complete the puzzle?

J   F   T   V

R   H   D   M

16   4   32   ?

IF 3 x 2 = 12

THEN

21 x 11 = ?

What is always part of a Wrick?

A. Straw

B. Metal

C. Candle grease

D. Music

E. Sprain

A dealer deals 10 cards – five red and five black mixed up. You have to pick a pair of red or black cards. Do the odds favour the dealer or you, or are the odds even?

S
E
C
T
I
O
N

12

119

• 1 • PUZZLE

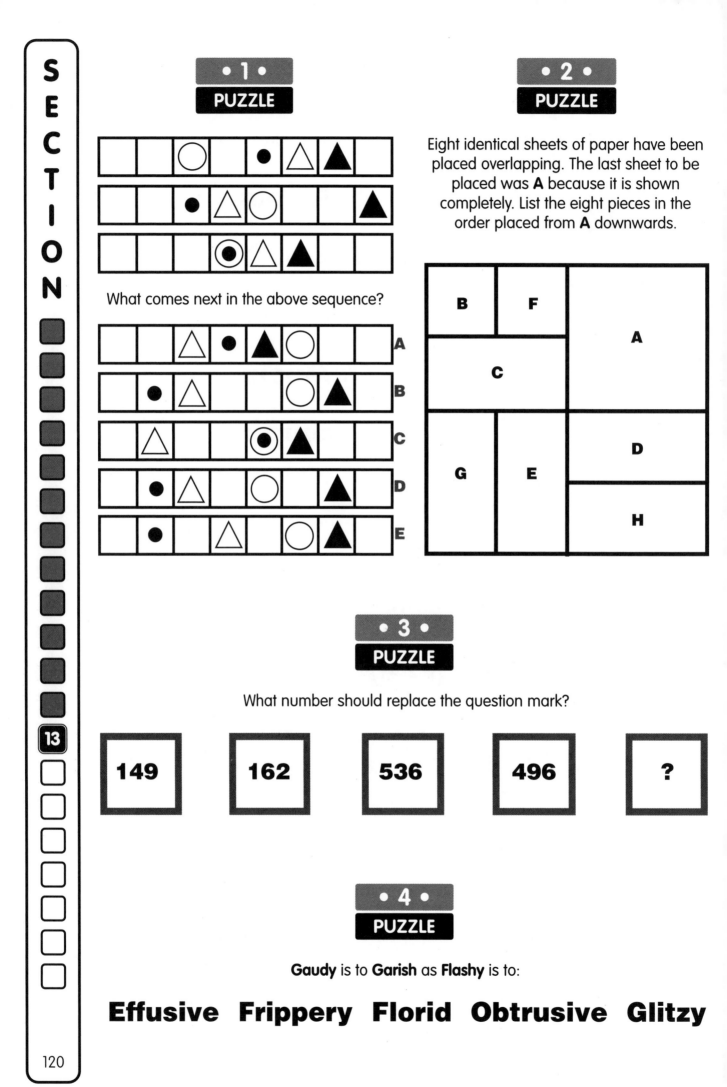

What comes next in the above sequence?

A
B
C
D
E

• 2 • PUZZLE

Eight identical sheets of paper have been placed overlapping. The last sheet to be placed was **A** because it is shown completely. List the eight pieces in the order placed from **A** downwards.

B F
C
A
G E
D
H

• 3 • PUZZLE

What number should replace the question mark?

149   162   536   496   ?

• 4 • PUZZLE

Gaudy is to **Garish** as **Flashy** is to:

Effusive   Frippery   Florid   Obtrusive   Glitzy

• 5 •
PUZZLE

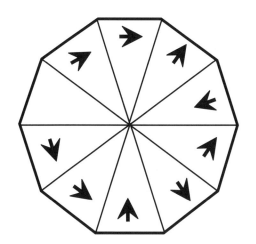

Which arrow goes in the empty segment?

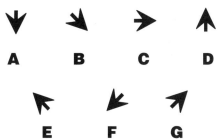

• 6 •
PUZZLE

4	8	3
2	7	2
1	3	5

is to

4	3	6
9	8	4
5	3	2

as

2	5	3
7	8	4
1	6	7

is to

4	5	8
6	9	7
3	8	2

as

7	4	6
2	8	1
4	3	5

is to

?	?	?
?	?	?
?	?	?

• 7 •
PUZZLE

What numbers should replace the question marks?

2	6
10	8
28	18
74	46
?	?

• 8 •
PUZZLE

Which word below is opposite to the word in capitals?

VALIANT

Withdrawn

Introvert

Craven

Sneaky

Unsuccessful

• 9 •
PUZZLE

What number should replace the question mark?

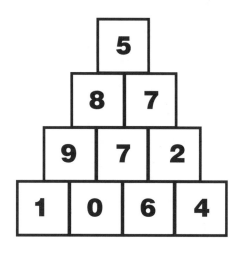

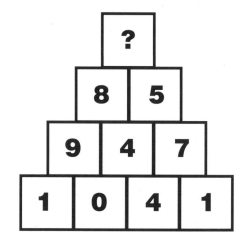

PUZZLE 10

A car travels 20 miles in the same time as another car travelling 20mph faster covers 30 miles. How long does the journey take?

PUZZLE 11

What number should replace the question mark?

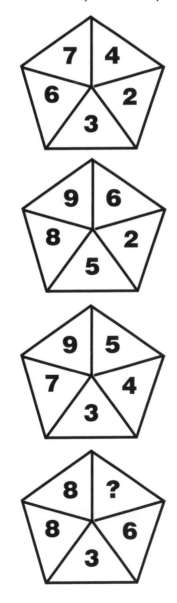

• 12 •
PUZZLE

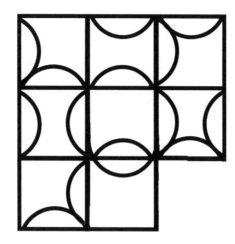

Which is the missing tile?

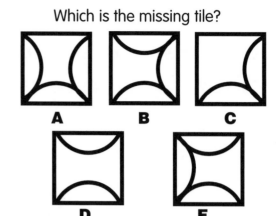

A   B   C

D   E

• 13 •
PUZZLE

Which letter should replace the question mark?

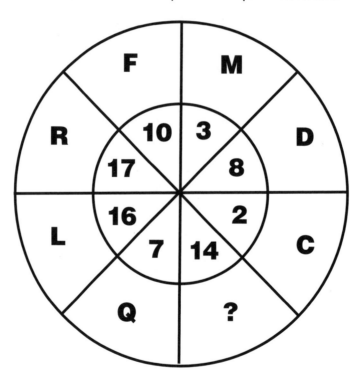

• 14 •
PUZZLE

Which is the odd one out?

Big Tall Large Bulky Massive

How many minutes is it before 12 noon, if 24 minutes ago it was 5 times as many minutes past 8am?

· 16 ·
PUZZLE

 is to

as is to

A

B

C

D

PUZZLE

Which number comes next?

| 7362 |
| 7368 |
| 7392 |
| 7398 |
| 7422 |
| 7430 |
| ? |

PUZZLE

Which letters should replace the question marks?

| AC | | CF | | EI | | GL | | ?? |

• 19 •
PUZZLE

What number should replace the question mark?

44
4 ? 25
23 6

15
5 8
7
18 31

• 20 • PUZZLE

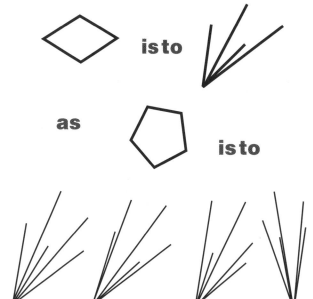

• 21 • PUZZLE

The number of dresses owned by Zoe is the same number owned by Linda divided by the number owned by Iris. Linda has 42 dresses and would own 8 times as many as Iris if Linda had 14 more. How many dresses does Zoe have?

• 22 • PUZZLE

What is suggested below?

DR. SMITH

OR

DR. JONES?

• 23 • PUZZLE

Which circle is nearest in content to **A**?

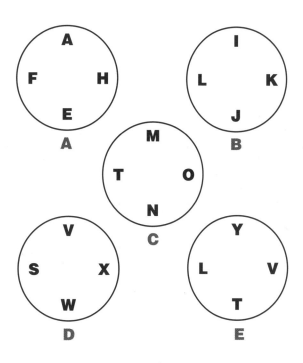

PUZZLE

How would you boil a three-minute egg with two egg-timers, one for five minutes, and one for eight minutes?

PUZZLE

Since my first birthday I have always had a birthday cake with the correct number of candles on it.

To date I have blown out 231 candles. How old am I?

PUZZLE

Which is the missing figure?

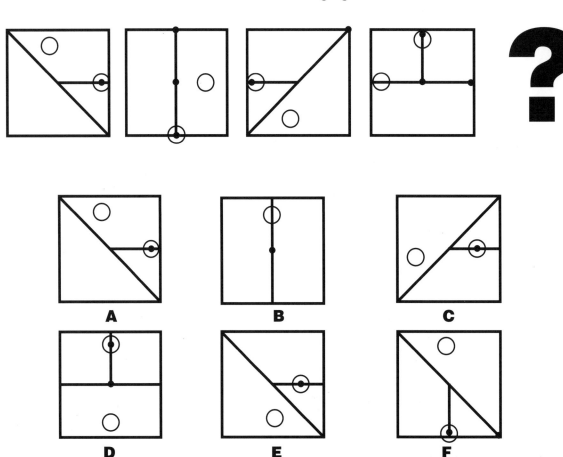

PUZZLE

Three tribes live on an island. The "Truers" always tell the truth. The "Fibbers" always lie. The "Trubers" make statements between truthfulness and falsehood. A said, "C is a Truer"; B said, "A is a Truber"; C said, "A is a Truer, and B is a Fibber".

To which tribes do A, B and C belong?

• 28 •
PUZZLE

Which circle is the odd one out?

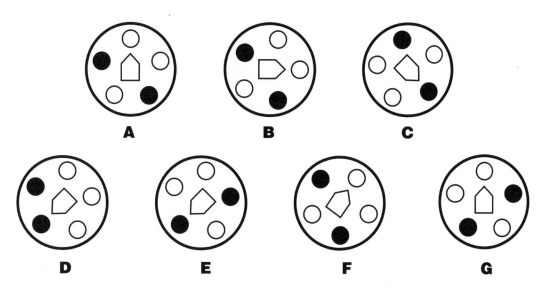

• 29 •
PUZZLE

What is the craving for Drinks?

A. Logo-mania

B. Keno-mania

C. Poto-mania

D. Photo-mania

E. Toxi-mania

• 30 •
PUZZLE

What would you always find in Guacamole?

A. Spinach

B. Turnips

C. Aniseed

D. Avocado

E. Pemmican

What letter should replace the question mark?

Which is the odd one out?

Apathy   Torpor   Inertia   Indolence   Idleness

Which number is the odd one out?

2358

3257

2246

4268

1459

3472   2134

3145

Which is the odd one out?

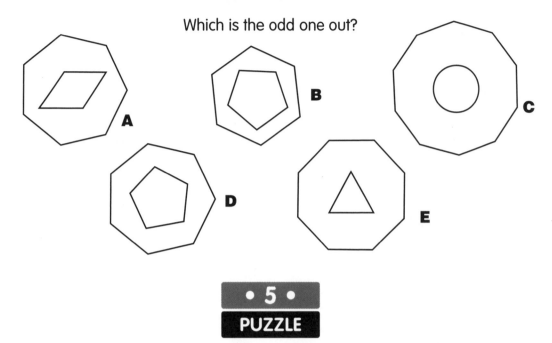

My neighbour returned from his orchard with a bag of apples. He gives to his wife half the apples plus half an apple, to my wife he gives half what he has left plus half an apple and to me he gives half what he has left plus half an apple. He then has no apples left.

How many apples did he bring back from the orchard originally?

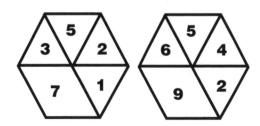

Which hexagon below is most like the hexagons above?

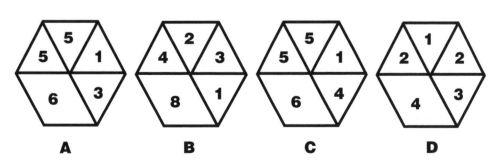

S
E
C
T
I
O
N

14

131

PUZZLE

Which word below means the same as the word in capitals?

QUAIL
Odd
Bird
Cringe
Brawl
Agonise

• 8 •
PUZZLE

How many lines appear below?

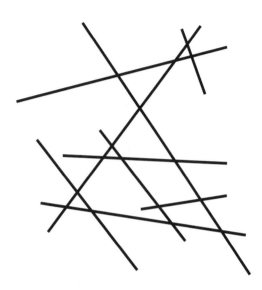

• 9 •
PUZZLE

What number is three places away from itself less 3, one place away from itself plus 2, two places away from itself less 5, one place away from itself less 4, three places away from itself less 6 and two places away from itself plus 4?

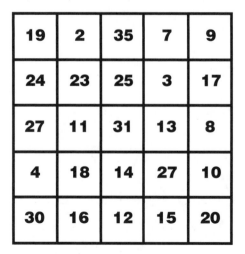

19	2	35	7	9
24	23	25	3	17
27	11	31	13	8
4	18	14	27	10
30	16	12	15	20

• 10 •
PUZZLE

Which three letters should replace the question marks?

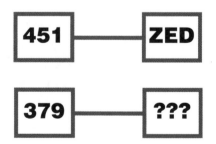

451 —— ZED

379 —— ???

Sierra is to **Mountains** as **Savannah** is to:

Desert Valley Grassland Inlet Swamp

Which is the missing tile?

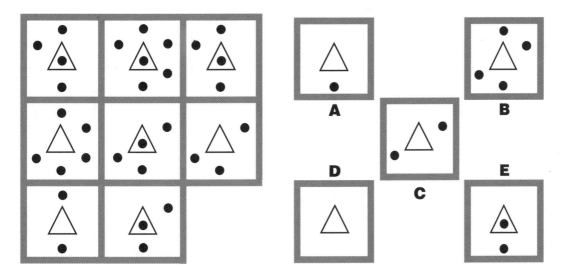

Out of 100 ladies surveyed, 82 had a black handbag, 65 had blue shoes, 68 carried an umbrella and 93 wore a ring. How many ladies, at least, must have had all four items?

• 14 •
PUZZLE

What numbers should replace the question marks?

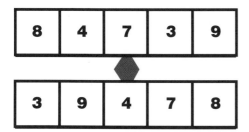

SECTION

14

133

PUZZLE 15

What is Pimiento?

A. Pepper

B. Horse

C. Colour

D. Head-dress

E. Religious devotion

PUZZLE 16

What number should replace the question mark?

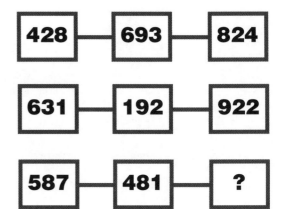

428 — 693 — 824

631 — 192 — 922

587 — 481 — ?

PUZZLE 17

Which of these cubes can be formed from this web?

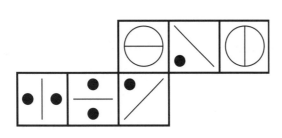

A   B   C

D   E

• 18 • PUZZLE

Make this equation true with one stroke of the pen.

6 + 6 + 6 = 652

• 19 • PUZZLE

What number should replace the question mark?

AHD	6
ESU	2
LCN	4
WOK	?

• 20 • PUZZLE

Which number is the odd one out?

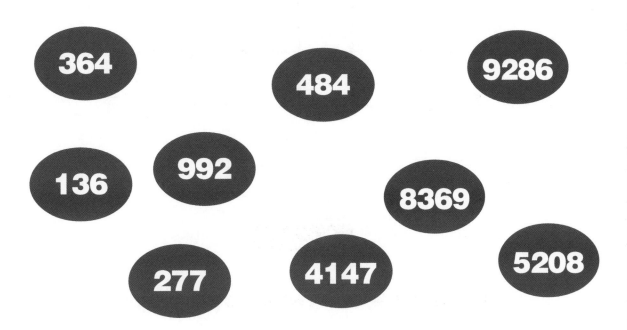

364   484   9286   136   992   8369   277   4147   5208

• 21 •
PUZZLE

$A + B = 27$
$B + C + D = 39$
$C + D = 27$
$D + E = 24$
$A + B + C + D + E = 65$

What is the value of **A, B, C, D, E**?

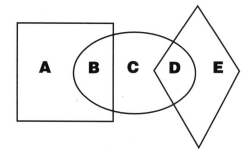

• 22 •
PUZZLE

Eight friends decide to meet at an intersection. To save too much walking where should they meet?

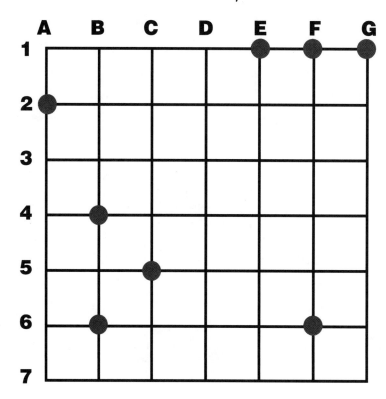

• 23 •
PUZZLE

IF 6 X 5 = 42 THEN 31 X 20 = ?

• 24 • PUZZLE

Which playing card replaces the question mark to complete the sequence?

• 25 • PUZZLE

IF

10 X 10 = 100

AND

10 + 10 = 100

THEN

101 + 1001 = ?

• 26 PUZZLE

Which two words mean the same?

Seraphic

Frivolous

Celestial

Puerile

Variety

Morose

• 27 • PUZZLE

What is obsession with the Sea?

A. Thalasso-mania

B. Hodo-mania

C. Gyno-mania

D. Grapho-mania

E. Dora-mania

SECTION

14

137

• 28 •
PUZZLE

Which figure will replace the question mark to complete the sequence?

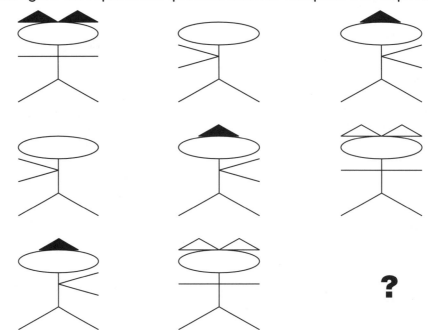

• 29 •
PUZZLE

Simplify:

17 - 8 x 2 + 17 x 3 - 6 = x

• 30 •
PUZZLE

Which letter replaces the question mark to complete the puzzle?

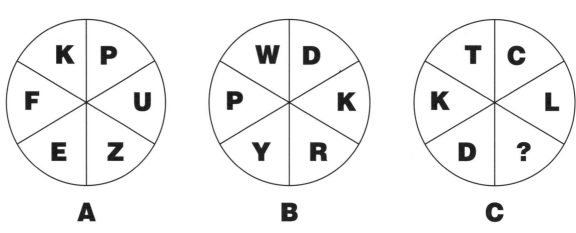

A

B

C

• 1 •
PUZZLE

What comes next in the above sequence?

A

B

C

D

E

F

• 2 •
PUZZLE

What time should appear on the fourth clock face?

| 9:37 | 10:14 | 10:51 | ? |

• 3 •
PUZZLE

A train travelling at a speed of 75mph enters a tunnel 1 1/4 miles long. The length of the train is 1/4 mile. How long does it take for all of the train to pass through the tunnel, from the moment the front enters to the moment the rear emerges?

PUZZLE

What number completes the grid, and where does it go?

		23			
	12			21	
			32		
	13				30
				41	
			12		

• 5 •
PUZZLE

Choose the missing tile from the options below.

A   B   C   D   E   F

PUZZLE • 6 •

Presto is to **Fast** as **Allegro** is to:

Slow Brisk Loud Soft Passionate

PUZZLE • 7 •

Which two letters should replace the question marks?

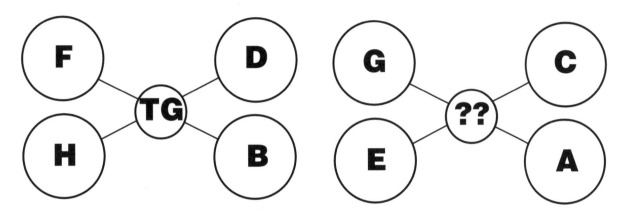

F
D G C
TG ??
H B E A

PUZZLE • 8 •

What number should replace the question mark?

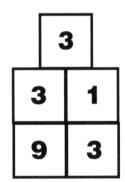

3	
3	1
9	3

2	
8	1
4	7

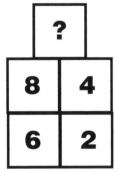

?	
8	4
6	2

PUZZLE • 9 •

Which two words are opposite in meaning?

Rugged Diligent Critical Practical Indifferent Resolute

PUZZLE • 10 •

How many lines appear below?

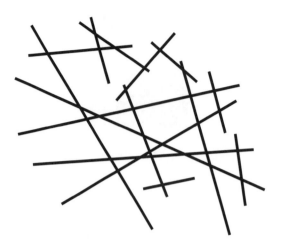

PUZZLE • 11 •

Each horizontal and vertical line contains the digits of a two-digit or three-digit square number. The digits are not necessarily adjacent in each line but are always in the correct order. Can you extract the 10 numbers? Every digit in the grid is used once each only.

1	1	3	2	1
9	8	6	4	3
1	6	2	3	9
6	2	5	6	6
4	1	4	9	1

PUZZLE • 12 •

What weight should replace the question mark in order to balance the scales?

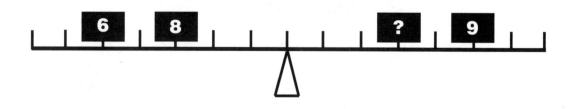

The cost of hiring a bus was shared equally by everyone who went on the outing. The bus was a twenty-seater and the bill came to $49.27. How many empty seats were there?

IF

4 X 3 = 22

THEN

14 X 4 = ?

Find the missing section from the four choices provided.

4	8	3	2	1	4	8	3
G	P	X	N	Q	G	P	X
4	1	2	3	8	4	1	2
G	Q	N	X	P	G	Q	N
8	3	2	1	4		3	2
P	X	N	Q				N
8	4	1	2	3		4	1
P	G	Q	N	X	P	G	Q
3	2	1	4	8	3	2	1

A

	3	
X	P	G
	4	

B

	2	
G	X	P
	2	

C

	8	
X	P	G
	8	

D

	8	
G	P	X
	8	

PUZZLE 16

Which is the odd one out?

Fictitious

Amazing

Mythical

Imaginary

Apocryphal

PUZZLE 17

What number should replace the question mark?

3	2	5	1
7	1	4	5
6	1	4	4
5	3	6	?

PUZZLE 18

Which number replaces the question mark to complete the sequence?

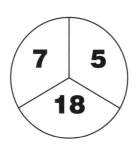
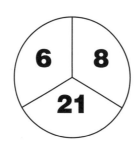
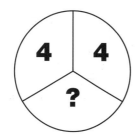

PUZZLE 19

Which letter should replace the question mark?

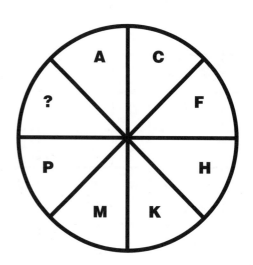

• 20 •
PUZZLE

How many minutes before 12 noon is it if 90 minutes later it will be as many minutes after 1pm?

• 21 •
PUZZLE

What number should replace the question mark?

(26) [6] (20³/₄) [13³/₄] (15¹/₂) [21¹/₂] (?)

• 22 •
PUZZLE

Against the wind a man could cycle at 15mph. With the wind a man could cycle at 20mph. How fast could he cycle on a calm day?

• 23 •
PUZZLE

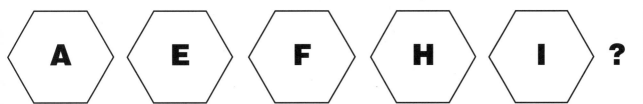

(A) (E) (F) (H) (I) ?

What letter below should replace the question mark?

(J) (K) (L)

• 24 •
PUZZLE

The end of the minute hand moves through 4.2" in 36mins. What is the length of the minute hand?

• 25 •
PUZZLE

Which number could replace the question mark?

22	4	8	6
6	4	15	15
12	15	27	?
4	23	4	2

• 26 •
PUZZLE

A servant is promised $1000 and a car for a year's services. After seven months he is fired and given $200 plus the car. What is the value of the car?

• 27 •
PUZZLE

The temperature at noon for five days was different and their product = 12°C.

What were the five temperatures?

PUZZLE

What is always part of a Paso Doble?

A. Hills B. Music

C. Sea D. Spanish fish E. Melons

PUZZLE

What is the meaning of Inequity?

A. Sadness B. Hesitation

C. Madness D. Bankruptcy

E. Unfairness

PUZZLE

Which playing card replaces the question mark to complete the sequence?

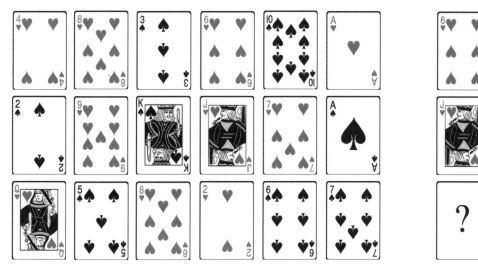

PUZZLE

What should replace the question marks?

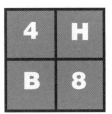

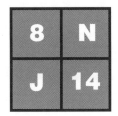

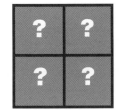

• 2 •
PUZZLE

The link between the numbers in each row is the same. Can you fill in the missing numbers?

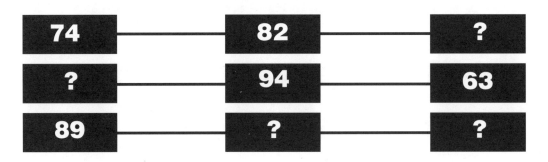

• 3 •
PUZZLE

Which is the odd one out?

Frisk
Gambol
Stampede
Frolic
Romp

• 4 •
PUZZLE

What number should replace the
question mark?

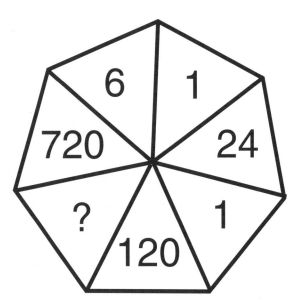

16

• 5 •
PUZZLE

What comes next in this sequence?

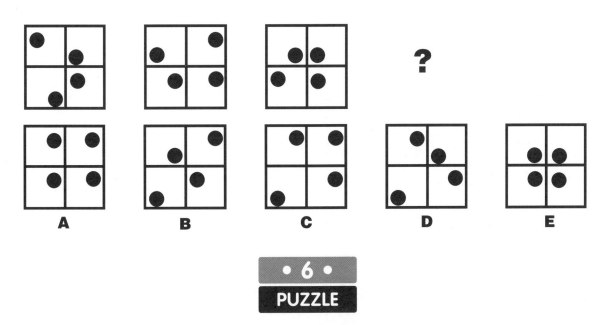

A   B   C   D   E

• 6 •
PUZZLE

What numbers should replace the question marks?

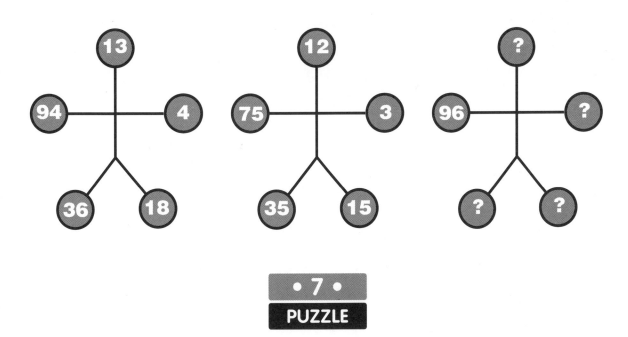

• 7 •
PUZZLE

Which two words are closest in meaning?

Expedition Crusade Challenge
Entrance Campaign Jaunt

PUZZLE • 8 •

Visit every square once each only to reach the treasure (T). 3S 1E means three squares South and one square East.

3S 1E	3E 4S	1S 2W	2W 1S	1S 2W
2S 2E	1W 2S	1N 2W	2S 1E	3W 1N
1N 4E	1N 2E	2N 1E	1E 2N	2W 2N
1N 3E	1E 1S	1W 1S	T	1S 1W
2N 1E	2N 1W	2N 2E	2N 1W	1N 1W

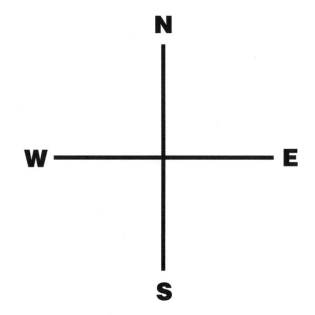

PUZZLE • 9 •

What time should replace the question mark?

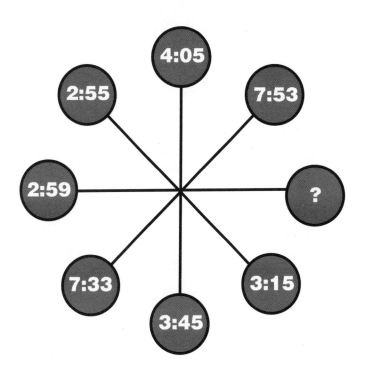

4:05
2:55
7:53
2:59
?
7:33
3:15
3:45

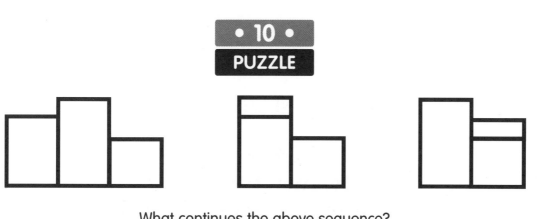

What continues the above sequence?

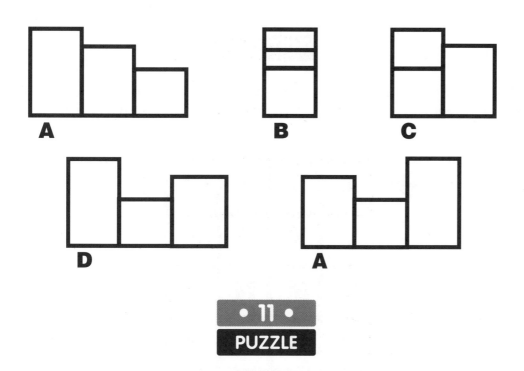

A   B   C

D   A

Which number should replace the question mark?

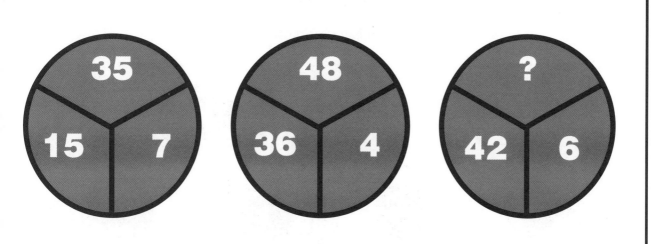

S
E
C
T
I
O
N

16

Octahedron is to Eight as Dodecahedron is to:

Ten
Twelve Sixteen
Twenty Twenty-Four

• 13 •
PUZZLE

Work from top left, from square to square horizontally or vertically, but not diagonally to unravel a logic sequence. Finish at the top right-hand square and use every square once each only.

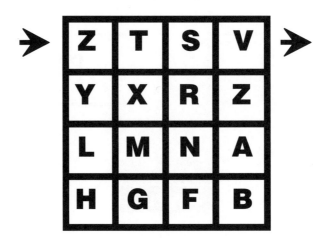

• 14 •
PUZZLE

Which is the odd one out?

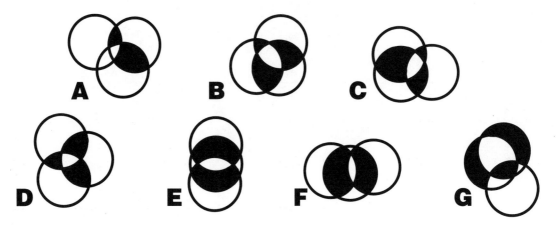

• 15 •
PUZZLE

What number should replace the question mark?

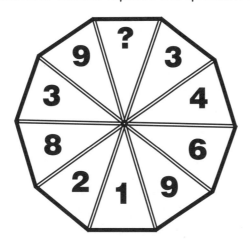

• 16 •
PUZZLE

How many minutes is it before 12 noon if 55 minutes ago it was four times as many minutes past 9am?

• 17 •
PUZZLE

Which Two Words Are Opposite In Meaning?

Important Haggard Momentary Fine Permanent Strong

• 18 •
PUZZLE

What number should replace the question mark?

| 13 | 21 | 27 | 45 | ? |

• 19 •
PUZZLE

To what number should the missing hand be pointing on the fifth clock face?

• 20 •
PUZZLE

Which numbers should replace the question marks?

2	3	4	6	9	12	18	36

2	3	4	6	8	12	?	?	32	48	96

• 21 •
PUZZLE

Which 4 letters should replace the question mark?

ABDC
JKML

DEGF
MNPO

GHJI
PQSR

JKML
?

• 22 •
PUZZLE

What is the missing figure?

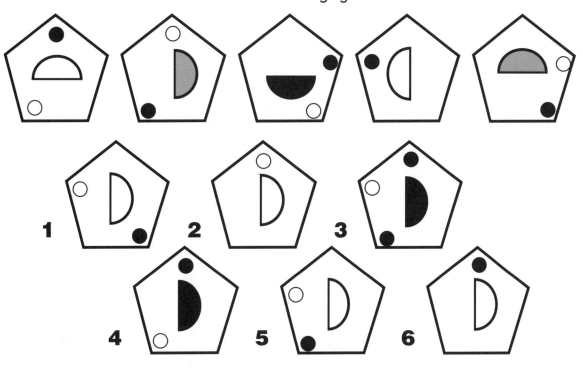

1   2   3

4   5   6

• 23 •
PUZZLE

Which of the following words:
Earthquake, Hurricane, Water spout, Thunder, or
Lightning should replace the question mark?

Breeze, Wind, Mistral, Chinook, ?

• 24 •
PUZZLE

What is the meaning of
Nubile?

A. Lissom
B. Marriageable
C. Young D. Slender
E. Clever

• 25 •
PUZZLE

What is the name given to
a group of Cats?

A. Clowder B. Nest
C. Howling D. Pack
E. Tide

16

• 26 •
PUZZLE

What is a Dotterel?
A. Fish
B. Bird
C. Animal
D. Insect
E. Flower

• 27 •
PUZZLE

Which of **A, B, C, D** or **E** fits into the blank circle to carry on a logical sequence?

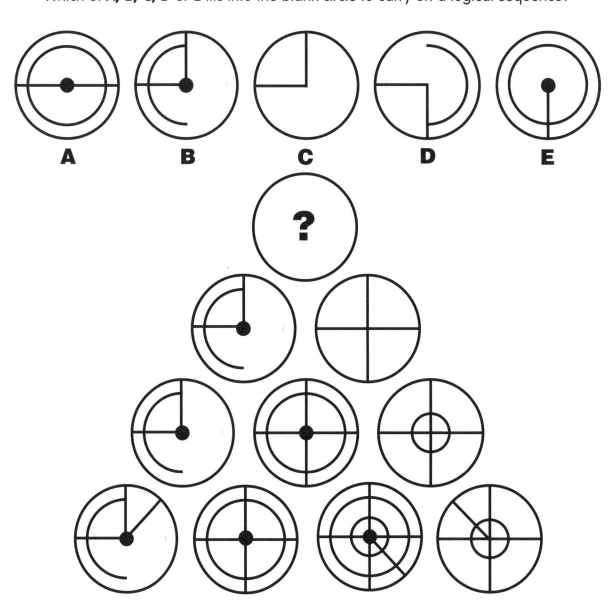

A   **B**   **C**   **D**   **E**

Which is the odd one out?

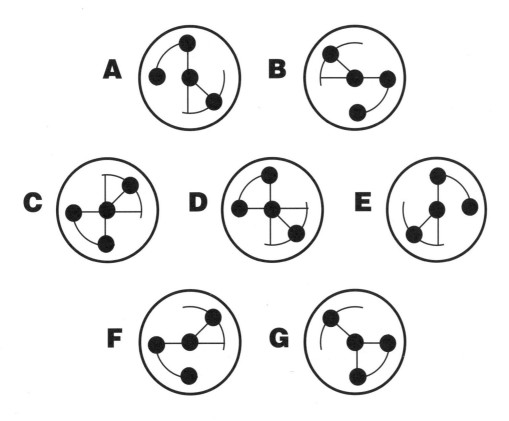

Foggy Hazy Misty Murky Smoky ?

Which word should replace the question mark?

Turbid Lucid Turgid Narrow Silent

Which two words are closest in meaning?

A. Exasperate
B. Truckle
C. Seize
D. Cringe
E. Fathom
F. Complain

S
E
C
T
I
O
N

16

• 1 •
PUZZLE

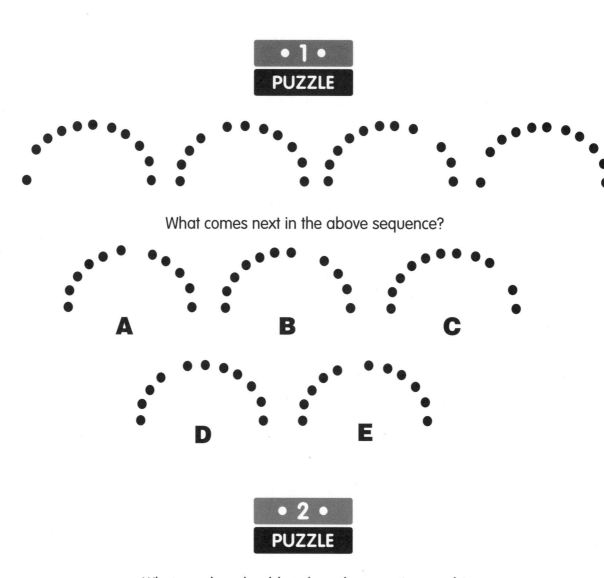

What comes next in the above sequence?

A   B   C

D   E

• 2 •
PUZZLE

What number should replace the question mark?

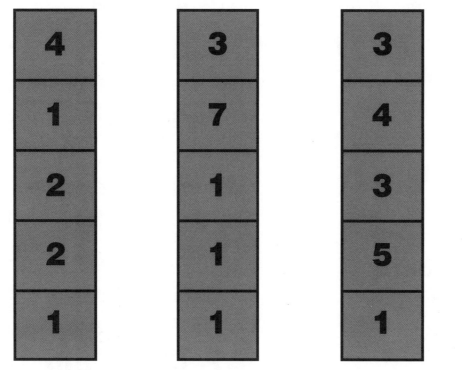

4	3	3	2
1	7	4	?
2	1	3	2
2	1	5	6
1	1	1	5

• 3 • PUZZLE

What letters should replace the question marks?

A	P	D	W	K	?
K	B	T	G	Y	?

• 4 • PUZZLE

What is Simian?

**A. Like-minded   B. Ape-like   C. Corrupt   D. Dark
E. Wise**

• 5 • PUZZLE

Which is the missing tile?

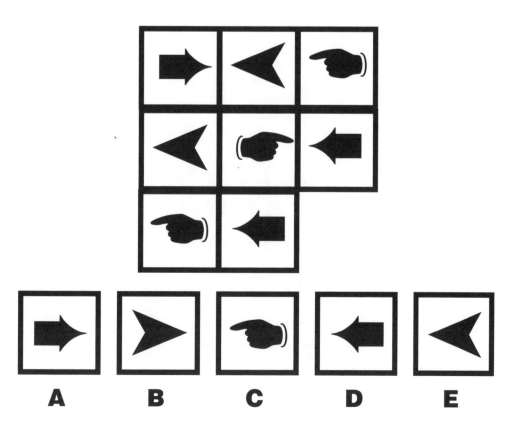

A   B   C   D   E

On glancing through your newspaper you notice that four pages are missing. One of the missing pages is page 8. The back page of the newspaper is 28.
What are the other three missing pages?

• 7 •
PUZZLE

What letter is two to the right of the letter three below the letter immediately to the right of the letter immediately above the letter two to the left of the letter O?

A	B	C	D	E
F	G	H	I	J
K	L	M	N	O
P	Q	R	S	T
U	V	W	X	Y	Z

• 8 •
PUZZLE

What number should replace the question mark?

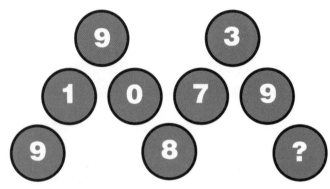

• 9 •
PUZZLE

Find the numbers.

```
    Q U I T
  X   N O W
  _____
    . . . . .
  . . . . . .
  _____
  T T T T T
```

• 10 •
PUZZLE

Which number in the grid appears twice, and which number from 1-81 is missing in the grid twice?

43	66	17	45	5	37	3	31	19
10	53	62	58	73	25	57	16	60
64	30	2	36	20	49	9	51	12
24	59	74	13	7	15	69	23	47
8	67	18	65	28	71	61	1	38
48	44	75	54	34	41	52	27	68
78	14	79	46	21	77	6	56	42
33	76	35	29	63	80	54	72	81
4	50	55	22	11	32	70	39	40

• 11 •
PUZZLE

Exalted is to Lofty as Expansive is to:

Stately   Magisterial   Rarefied   Sublime   Lavish

• 12 •
PUZZLE

3684 is to **91412**

as  **7196** is to:

(a) 98226
(b) 81015
(c) 30142
(d) 61014

PUZZLE • 13 •

How thick should a coin have to be, to be spun and have a 1 in 3 chance of landing on its edge?

PUZZLE • 14 •

A man is walking his dog on the lead towards home at a steady 4 mph. When they are 5 miles from home the man lets his dog off the lead. The dog immediately runs off towards home at 8 mph. When the dog reaches the house it turns round and runs back to the man at the same speed. This is repeated until the man gets home and lets in the dog.
How many miles does the dog cover from being let off the lead to being let in the house?

PUZZLE • 15 •

What number should replace the question mark?

	16	
36	12	12
	9	

	16	
15	8	17
	4	

	20	
18	?	22
	5	

PUZZLE • 16 •

Which is the odd one out?

Pensive
Serene
Reflective
Meditative
Contemplative

• 17 •
PUZZLE

How many lines appear below?

• 18 •
PUZZLE

Which row of numbers is the odd one out?

A	6	4	7	1	2	5
B	8	4	6	3	2	5
C	1	4	6	2	3	8
D	7	5	8	2	3	6
E	2	5	7	3	4	9

• 19 •
PUZZLE

Which number should replace the question mark?

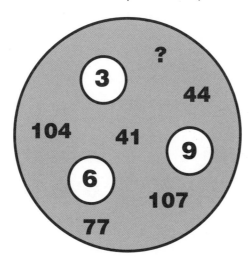

• 20 •
PUZZLE

A farmer sold three sheep and bought two pigs, but was $20 out of pocket. He then sold two sheep and bought one pig, and this time broke even exactly. All the sheep had the same sale price and all the pigs the same cost.

What was the cost of a pig and the price of a sheep?

• 21 •
PUZZLE

What is the obsession with Mirrors?

A. Katoptro-mania
B. Astero-mania
C. Tremo-mania
D. Grapho-mania
E. Scio-mania

• 22 •
PUZZLE

Which two words are the opposite to each other?

A. Injunction
B. Unfair
C. Inimitable
D. Intimation
E. Inhibition
F. Comparable

• 23 •
PUZZLE

What is always part of a Volute?

A. Spiral
B. Parchment
C. Cloud
D. Club
E. Animal

• 24 •
PUZZLE

Which two words are the opposite to each other?

Assuage
Affirm
Maintain
Impose
Agree
Aggravate

Which could be a Cantata?

A. Fruit
B. Vegetable
C. Cocktail
D. Opera
E. Psalm

What is always a part of Virelay?

A. Fireplace
B. Dark road
C. Sea nymph
D. Stanza
E. Troglodyte

Arrange the following 12 creatures in sets of four.
The 3 sets are:

4 Insects, 4 Birds, 4 Animals

Panda	Bushbaby	Perchary
	Cachalot	
Emmet	Slug	Fulmar
	Moth	
Woodlice	Hornbill	Shelduck
	Aardvark	

• 28 •
PUZZLE

What is always part of a Couchette?

A. A vegetable B. Liver C. A sleeping berth D. Semolina E. Nectar

• 29 •
PUZZLE

An oxymoron is a linking of contradictory terms.
Find 6 oxymorons.

Non-Dairy   Homeless   Odds
III   Savant
Even   Idiot   Health
Light   Creamer
Shelter   Night

• 30 •
PUZZLE

We have 100 sweets in five bowls.
1st and 2nd = 52
2nd and 3rd = 43
3rd and 4th = 34
4th and 5th = 30

How many sweets in each bowl?

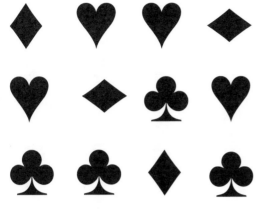

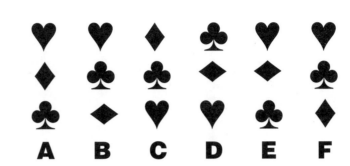

What continues this sequence?

What number should replace the question mark?

0   1   5   ?   30   55

A farmer has 200 yards of fencing and wishes to enclose a rectangular area of the greatest possible size. What will be its area?

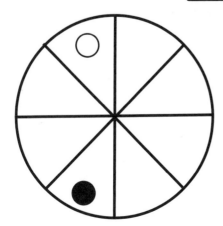

At each stage the dot moves one segment anti-clockwise and the circle moves two spaces anti-clockwise. After how many stages do the two appear in the same segment?

• 5 •
PUZZLE

What number should replace the question mark?

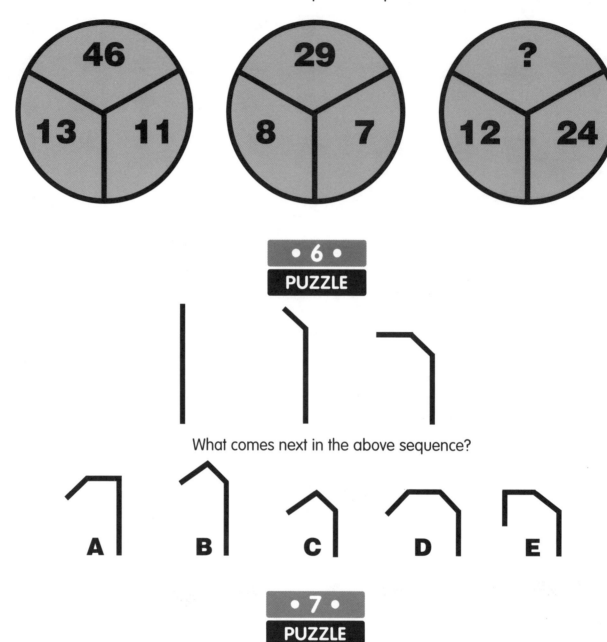

• 6 •
PUZZLE

What comes next in the above sequence?

A B C D E

• 7 •
PUZZLE

What number should replace the question mark?

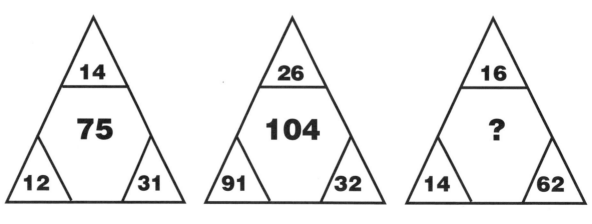

14
75
12   31

26
104
91   32

16
?
14   62

• 8 • PUZZLE

Which is the odd one out?
Nabob
Mogul
Magistrate
Tycoon
Magnate

• 9 • PUZZLE

What number should replace the question mark?

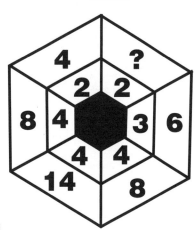

• 10 • PUZZLE

What number should replace the question mark?

2581	—	95
4916	—	47
?	—	68

• 11 • PUZZLE

What comes next in the sequence?

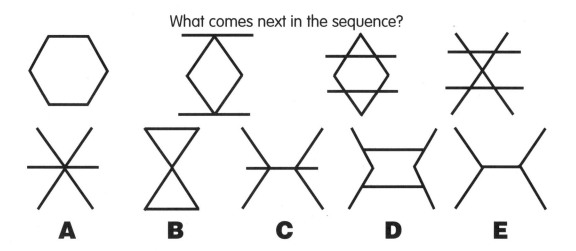

A   B   C   D   E

• 12 •
PUZZLE

What comes next?

d, H, E

A   B   C   D   E

• 13 •
PUZZLE

Which letter should replace the question mark?

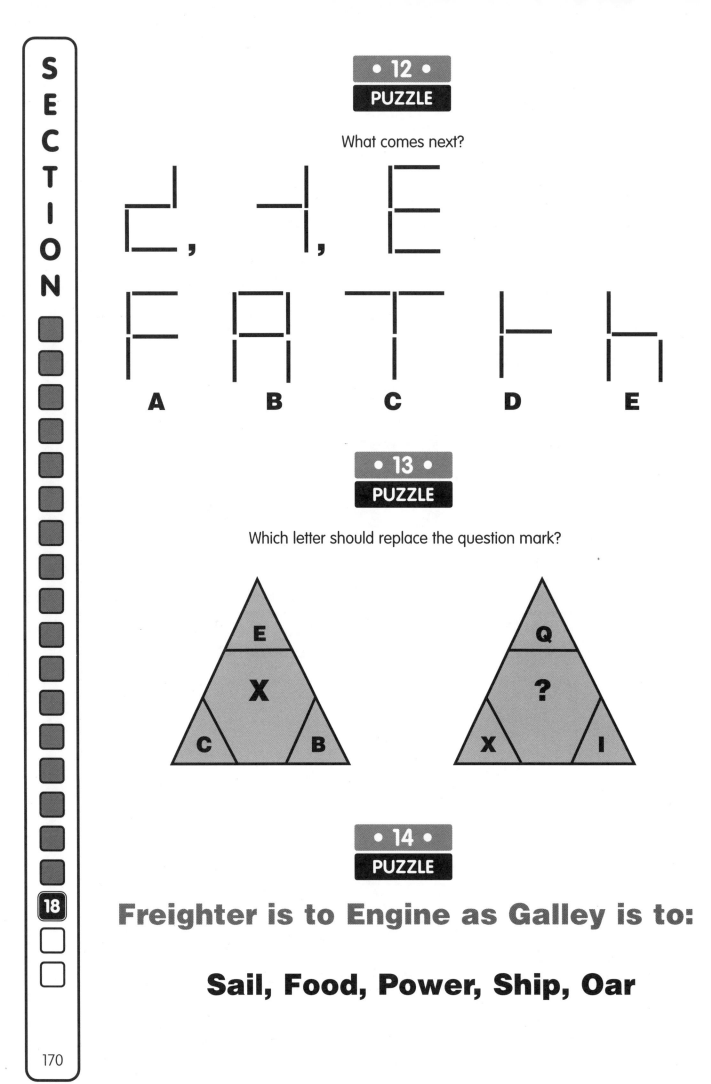

• 14 •
PUZZLE

Freighter is to Engine as Galley is to:

Sail, Food, Power, Ship, Oar

is to

as:

is to:

A   B   C   D   E

What number should replace the question mark?

SECTION

18

• 17 •
PUZZLE

A car manufacturer produces only blue and white models which come out of the final testing area completely at random. What are the odds that three consecutive cars of the same colour will come through the test area at any one time?

• 18 •
PUZZLE

Which clock face is the odd one out?

| A 12:33:45 | B 16:41:57 |

C 18:26:44

| D 16:37:51 | E 25:28:53 |

• 19 •
PUZZLE

Which is the odd one out?

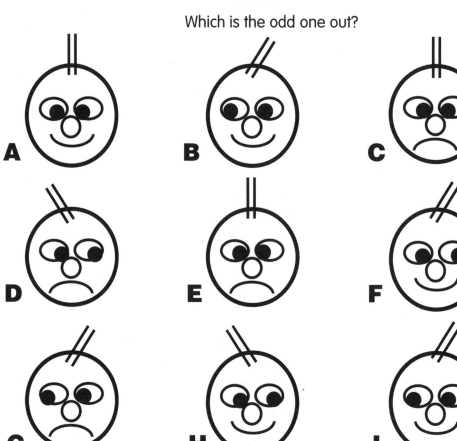

A B C

D E F

G H I

Can you correctly fill in the missing numbers?

4	7	3	1	6	8	4	7	3
1	6	8	4	7	3	1	6	8
3	8	6	7	4	1	3	8	6
8	3	7	?	?	4	8	3	7
6	1	4	?	?	7	6	1	4
7	4	1	3	8	6	7	4	1
4	7	3	1	6	8	4	7	3
1	6	8	4	7	3	1	6	8

What number should replace the question mark?

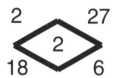
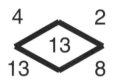
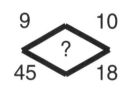
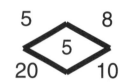

Find the value for x

$$\frac{117}{169} = x$$

• 23 • PUZZLE

These 12 words will make 6 pairs which go together.

PIN
SNAPS
CHURCH
MOUSE
SWEEP
CHIMNEY
MATE
CUSHION
BRANDY
FOX
HOUNDS
STALE

• 24 • PUZZLE

What is a Noctule?

A. A hawk
B. A dormouse
C. A cube of meat
D. A bat E. A boat

• 25 • PUZZLE

Which two words mean the same?
Limpid Unruly
Lascivious Baleful
Adroit Pellucid

• 26 • PUZZLE

The mileage gauge on the car was showing a palindromic number:

1 5 9 5 1

Only after two hours did it show another palindromic number.

What was it?

• 27 • PUZZLE

What number should replace the question mark?

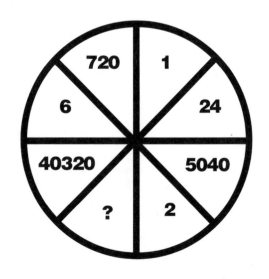

720 1
6 24
40320 5040
? 2

• 28 •
PUZZLE

Simplify:

$$\frac{3}{8} \div \frac{15}{24} = x$$

• 29 •
PUZZLE

There are 9 stations from Town A to Town B. How many different single tickets must be printed so that one may book from any station to any other?

• 30 •
PUZZLE

Which diagram should replace the question mark?

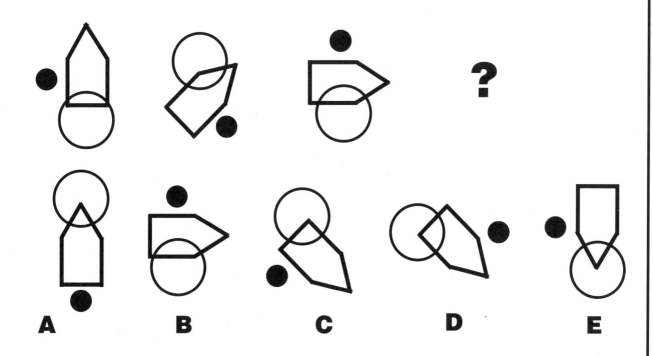

A **B** **C** **D** **E**

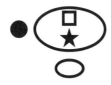

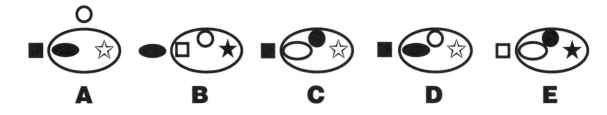

What continues the above sequence?

A   B   C   D   E

PUZZLE 2

Hautboy is to Oboe as Sackbut is to:

Bagpipe
Trombone
Flute
Tuba
Horn

PUZZLE 3

Which number should replace the question mark?

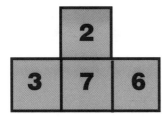

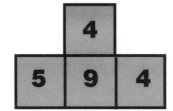

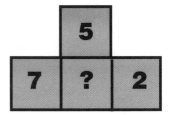

• 4 •
PUZZLE

What number should replace the question mark?

342	7055	136
236	9563	272
168	**?**	235

• 5 •
PUZZLE

A car crashes and witnesses who run to the scene immediately find the driver dead slumped over the steering wheel in his car with an arrow sticking out of his back. All the car doors and windows are locked and it is obvious that no-one has entered or tampered with the car, and that he was completely alone in the car.

How did he die?

• 6 •
PUZZLE

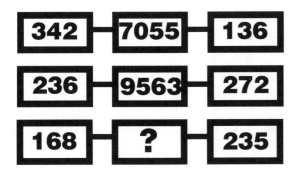

What comes next in the above sequence?

A   **B**   **C**   **D**   **E**

• 7 •
PUZZLE

Which is the odd one out?

Mandolin, Trumpet, Lute, Viola, Sitar

PUZZLE

Which number should replace the question mark?

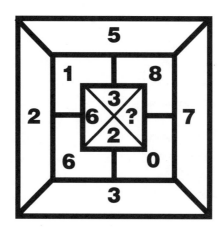

PUZZLE

Which letter should replace the question mark?

PUZZLE

Which word in brackets means the same as the word in capitals?

LUCID
(Timely, Fruitful, Sparkling, Limpid, Smooth)

• 11 •
PUZZLE

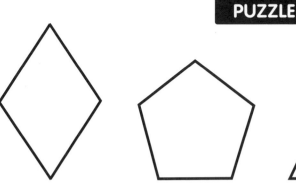  

What comes next in the above sequence?

A   **B**   **C**   **D**

E   **F**   **G**

• 12 •
PUZZLE

Which word in brackets is opposite to the word in capitals?

CHASTE
(Careful, Wanton, Hunted, Modest, Mean)

PUZZLE 13

What number should replace the question mark?

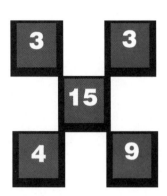 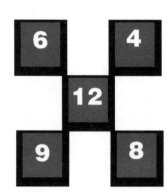 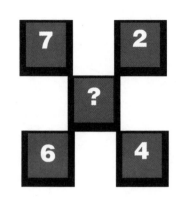

PUZZLE 14

Which number should replace the question mark?

7639

6867

4802

?

PUZZLE 15

What is Faïence?

A. Architecture
B. Folk song
C. Furniture
D. Painting on wood
E. Pottery

· 16 ·
PUZZLE

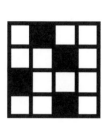  

Which box continues the sequence?

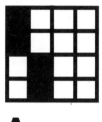 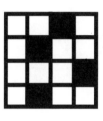   

A   **B**   **C**   **D**   **E**

· 17 ·
PUZZLE

Insert the numbers 1-8 in the circles so the sum of all connecting circles is the same as the value given in the table below.

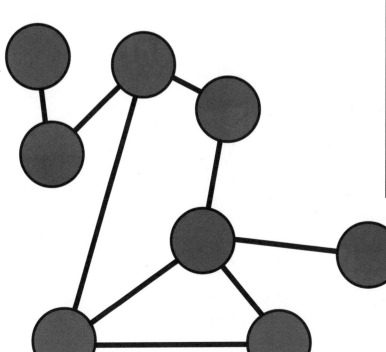

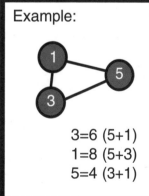
Example:

3=6 (5+1)
1=8 (5+3)
5=4 (3+1)

1=21	5=7
2=17	6=3
3=1	7=7
4=11	8=5

19

PUZZLE

What should replace the question mark?

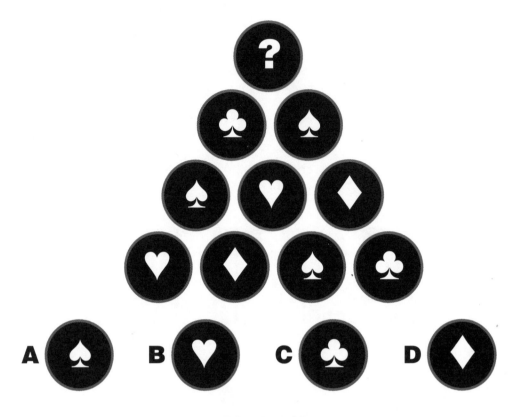

A   B   C   D

• 19 •
PUZZLE

What number should replace the question mark?

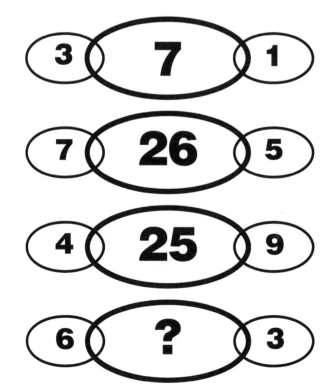

• 20 •
PUZZLE

In the addition sum below only two of the decimal points are in the correct place.

Correct three of the decimal points to make the calculation correct.

56.843
1.29
168.72
5.638
_____

1313.85

• 21 •
PUZZLE

These 12 words will go together to make up 6 pairs of words.

**Charm   Staff
Walk   Wishing
Garden   Board
Gnome   Lucky
Liner   Well   Car
Ocean**

• 22 •
PUZZLE

Which two words mean the same?

**Insidious
Dishonest
Detestation
Discordance
Disingenuous
Dismay**

• 23 •
PUZZLE

What is the name given to a group of Rooks?

**A. Building
B. Murder
C. Budget
D. Exaltation
E. Flight**

• 24 •
PUZZLE

What phrase is suggested below?

ECNALG

• 25 •
PUZZLE

In a class of 40 children, 20 can play table tennis and 25 can play soccer.
5 cannot play either table tennis or soccer.

How many children can play both table tennis and soccer?

• 26 •
PUZZLE

Which number should replace the question mark?

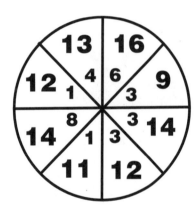

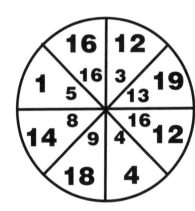

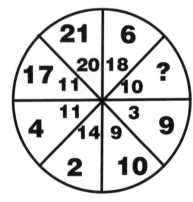

• 27 •
PUZZLE

Simplify:

$$\frac{7}{8} \div \frac{49}{64} = x$$

These 12 words will go together to make 6 pairs.

Foot	**Dance**	**Frame**	**Tap**
Picture	**Beer**	**Candle**	**Ginger**
Hat	**Grease**	**Loose**	**Stand**

Which two words are opposite in meaning?

**Fain Fallacy Fright Unwilling
Erroneous Ready**

What is always part of Cointreau?

A. Peppermint
B. Orange
C. Lemon
D. Lime
E. Olives

PUZZLE •1•

What comes next in this sequence?

 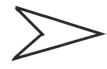

 **A**   **B**    **C**

 D   **E**   **F**

PUZZLE •2•

What number should replace the question mark?

PUZZLE •3•

What number should replace the question mark?

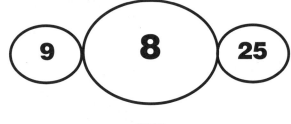

9   8   25

| 1 | 3 | 2 | 4 | ? | 5 |

36   ?   49

• 4 • PUZZLE

Which two words are closest in meaning?

Animal Beseech Pray Target Weapon Help

• 5 • PUZZLE

What number should replace the question mark?

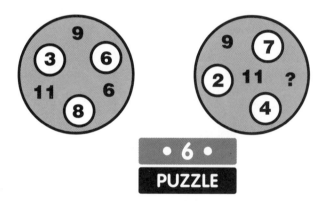

• 6 • PUZZLE

Which is the odd one out?

PUZZLE 7

What number should replace the question mark?

793582

676

?

32

PUZZLE 8

What number should replace the question mark?

2	7	9
5	7	7
3	8	2
4	3	1
7	2	9
?	2	2

PUZZLE 9

Which is the odd one out?

Rugby
Soccer
Cricket
Swimming
Water-Polo

Which is the missing tile?

A   B   C   D   E

F   G   H

What number should replace the question mark?

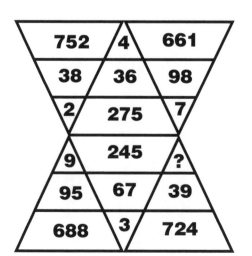

The link between the numbers in each row is the same. Can you fill in the missing numbers?

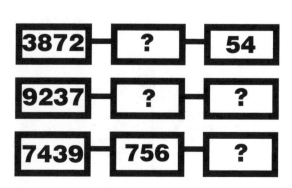

S
E
C
T
I
O
N

20

189

• 13 •

PUZZLE

What number should replace the question mark?

• 14 •

PUZZLE

Which box continues the sequence?

 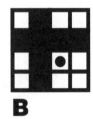   

A   **B**   **C**   **D**   **E**

• 15 •

PUZZLE

What numbers should replace the question marks?

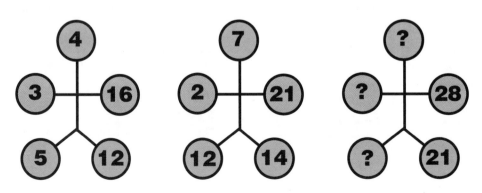

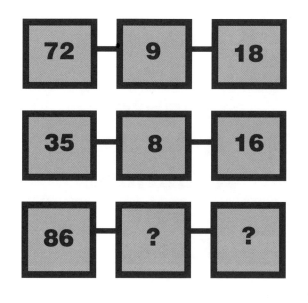

• 16 •
PUZZLE

Which numbers should replace the question marks?

72	9	18
35	8	16
86	?	?

• 17 •
PUZZLE

What should replace the question mark
A, B, C, D or **E**?

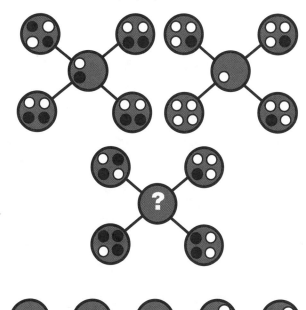

A   B   C   D   E

• 18 •
PUZZLE

Two men run a race of 100 metres which man 'A' wins by 5 metres. Because of this the next race is handicapped, and man 'A' stands 5 metres behind the line, thereby giving man 'B' 5 metres start. They both run the second race at exactly the same speed as before.

What is the result?

• 19 •
PUZZLE

What number should replace the
question mark?

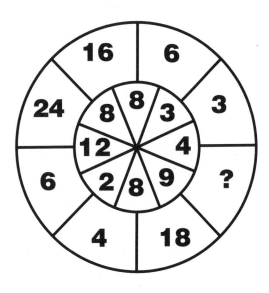

• 20 •
PUZZLE

Chemistry is to Substances as Fauna is to:

Plants
Animals
Reactions
Soil
Rocks

• 21 •
PUZZLE

**The name of which fish is
indicated below?**

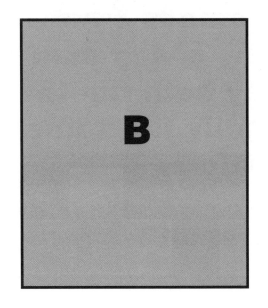

• 22 •
PUZZLE

**Three men in
succession toss a coin.
The winner is the first
to throw a head.**

**A goes 1st
B goes 2nd
C goes 3rd**

**What are their
chances?**

• 23 • PUZZLE

Five suspects have been interrogated.

Who is the culprit, if two of the statements below are false?

Alan said, "Dan is the culprit."
Bob said, "I am not guilty."
Charles said, "It was not Eddie."
Dan said, "Alan lies when he says that I did it."
Eddie said, "Bob is telling the truth."

• 24 • PUZZLE

A sphere and a cone can be fitted exactly into a cylinder separately.

What are ratios of the three volumes?

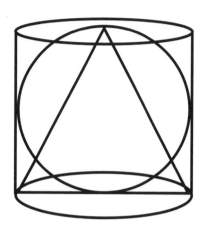

• 25 • PUZZLE

Find out what letter replaces the question mark?

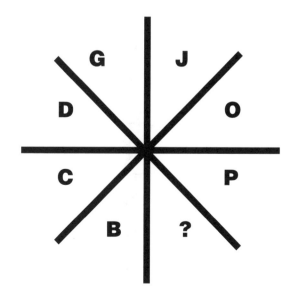

• 26 • PUZZLE

These 12 words will make up 6 pairs of words which go together.

Parlour   Cup
Penny   Teddy
Whistle   Gang
Bear   Chain
Train   Maid
Hook   Steam

Which two words are opposite in meaning?

Intrigue
Renounce
Derogate
Appreciate
Define
Eligible

What is always part of Handsel?

A. Vegetable
B. Drink
C. Coin
D. Weed
E. Maiden

Simplify:

$$\frac{19}{26} \div \frac{38}{52} = X$$

Solve the cryptarithm

```
        EEO
  X      OO
      ‾‾‾‾‾‾
      EOEO
      EOO
    ‾‾‾‾‾‾‾
    OOOOO
```

Each E stands for an even digit
Each O stands for an odd digit
Not necessarily the same digit

SOLUTIONS

SECTION 1

1 – E
Looking across each line and down each column, the diamond rotates 45° anti-clockwise at each stage.

2 – J
A–C skips 1 letter, C–F skips 2, then skip 3 letters from F.

3 – 13
In each row of 3 circles the number in the middle circle is the sum of all the odd numbers in the circles either side.

4 – R
Start at A and work clockwise including only letters which have enclosed areas when printed.

5 – Facile, Difficult

6 – 8547
In the others multiply the first and fourth numbers to obtain the middle two digits.

7 – E
In the others the min/sec figure is 0.75 of the hour figure. (12.75 = 12 3/4; 8.25 = 8 1/4, etc.)

8 – D
The others are the same figure rotated.

9 – Desk

10 – D
Taking numerical positions in the alphabet, in the others the middle letter is the sum of the other two.

11 – Treble
It is a clef, the others are notes.

12 – 364
Multiply numbers by 3 and add 1.

13 – NMG
At each stage reverse the letters and discard the letter 3rd from end.

14 – 11

15 – Altruistic, Selfish

16 – 170
In each column, take their respective numerical position in the alphabet, multiply letter at top by letter at bottom to obtain the middle number in the first column, then divide in the second, etc.

17 – 4
Opposite sides of dice total 7. The total of 13 dice is, therefore, 91 (13 x 7). As 39 is showing, this leaves 91 - 39 = 52 on the reverse, an average of 52/13 = 4.

18 – 6
Looking across and down the sum of alternate numbers in each line and column are equal.

19 – I drove the car in reverse.

20 – 3

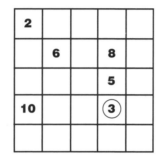

21 – A

22 – D

23 – C

24 – $\frac{7}{8} \times \frac{24}{14} = 1\frac{1}{2}$

25 – x = -22½
Order must be taken x, ÷, +, -

26 – Parabola

27 – 0.875
From top to bottom, each number represents the fractions 1/2, 2/3, 3/4, 4/5, 5/6, 6/7 and 7/8.

28 – 6
The 3 sectors in the same position add up to 20.

29 – 46
Modulo 9
6x5 (Modulo 10) = (3x10)+(0x1) = 30
6x5 (Modulo 9) = (3x9) + (3x1) = 33
7x6 (Modulo 10) = (4x10) + (6x1) = 42
7x6 (Modulo 9) = (4x9) + (6x1) = 46

30 – 64
In each square, multiply pairs of numbers which are diagonally opposite each other and calculate their difference to give the value in the centre.

SECTION 2

1 – 6
Reading from left to right, top row to bottom, the digits represent the number of letters in each word of the question.

2 – Manifest, Evident

3 – V, Z
Working clockwise, the letters in the first triangle jump one place in the alphabet, in the second they jump two, therefore, in the third they jump three.

4 – 11
In each column the largest number is the sum of all the odd numbers in that column.

5 – 8
Working round the horseshoe from A, substitute letters for numbers according to their position in the alphabet. Each letter or number is the sum of the previous two letters or numbers i.e. 3 + 5 (E) = 8.

6 – G
Every other square has a mirror image pairing.

7 – Scapula
This is part of the arm, the others are part of the leg.

8 – 3.82
  69.4
   1.246
  <u>18.37</u>
 92.836

9 – Milk

10 – 89
Starting on the left, square each seperate digit from the 2 digit numbers and add the squares together to give the next number along., i.e. $7^2 + 4^2 = 49 + 16 = 65$.

11 – 10lbs
50/5 = 10

12 – B
The outer arc moves 90° clockwise; the middle arc moves 180°; the inner arc moves 90° anti-clockwise.

13 – C

195

SOLUTIONS

14 – 382
The rest have an anagram pairing
784-478, 329-932, 526-652, 397-793, 894-489

15 – Edify, Educate

16 – B
The circle turns to an ellipse and goes inside the rectangle, which becomes a square.

17 – 468137
The even numbers from the first number in ascending order, followed by the odd numbers.

18 – 47 appears twice, 34 is missing.

19 – FD
According to their position in the alphabet they are ascending square numbers: 16, 25, 36, 49, 64

20 – C

21 – 11
Add together numbers in corresponding segments of circles A and B and put the result in circle C.

22 – $\frac{7}{32} \times \frac{16}{14} = \frac{1}{4}$

23 $\frac{1}{1.155}$ = 52 mins

2hrs	Take reciprocal	$\frac{1}{2}$ = 0.5
3hrs	→	$\frac{1}{3}$ = 0.33
5hrs	→	$\frac{1}{5}$ = 0.2
8hrs	→	$\frac{1}{8}$ = 0.125

Add fractions together → 1.155
Calculate reciprocal of 1.155

24 – B
Horizontal top line and right-hand vertical line remain still. While, horizontal bottom line and left hand vertical line moves 1/2 right and 1/2 up.

25 – B

26 – C

27 – D
The 2 lower circles combine to produce the circle above but like symbols disappear.

28 – B

29 – KM

30 – $-6\frac{1}{2}$
There are 2 sequences: $-5\frac{1}{2}$, $+5\frac{1}{2}$

SECTION 3

1 – June

2 – 27
Start at 4 and work along the top line then back along the second line etc, adding 8 then subtracting 5.

3 – MH
Start at AZ and work clockwise jumping to alternate segments. Jump 1 forward from A and 2 back from Z.

4 – The calculations would still be correct if the multiplication signs were substituted by plus signs.

5 – E
Looking across add the circles in the first two squares to obtain the number of circles in the final square. Looking down, deduct instead of add.

6 – 4
The number represents the number of straight lines in the letter.

7 – Honour

8 – 13
The numbers in the outer pentagon are the sum of the two numbers directly opposite in the inner pentagon.

9 – Chess
The rest are card games.

10 – He was born in hospital room 1969 and died in room 1999.

11 – D
So that there are two dots in just one circle and one dot in two circles.

12 – M
The letter appears in the overlapping segments that only appears once in the two rectangles.

13 – D

14 – DEC
The letters following the top letter in each rectangle follow in the same order in each rectangle.

15 – D
The contents of each hexagon is determined by the two hexagons below them. Only when 2 circles of the same colour appear in the same position are they carried forward, but black circles change to white and vice versa.

16 – 35.35
Reverse and add,
i.e. 13.22 + 22.13 = 35.35

17 – Chant

18 – 9
Add 1, 2, 3, 4, 5, 6 in turn to the numbers in the first rectangle.

19 – Mrs. Brown
Gill, Brown, Green, Jones

20 – UVWXY
Increase number of letters by 1 each time in the sequence
A(B)CD(EF)GHI(JKL)MNO
P(QRST)UVWXY

21 – 303 132
They are running numbers 21-22-23 etc.

22 – 184
There were 132 men and 68 women.
132 x $\frac{1}{11}$ = 12
68 x $\frac{1}{17}$ = 4
Therefore there were 16 in prison.

23 – Bermuda, Formosa, Madeira

24 – R
The letters are the last ones used when the numbers are written out in English i.e. fifteeN, one hundreD etc.

25 – 7
In each triangle, calculate the sum of the three outer numbers, then reverse the digits to give the central number. (18+7+11=36, reversed =63)

26 – E
8 dots

27 – 44
Modulo 8
4x4 (Modulo 10) = (1x10) + (6x1) = 16
4x4 (Modulo 8) = (2x8) + (0x1) = 20
6x6 (Modulo 10) = (3x10) + (6x1) = 36
6x6 (Modulo 8) = (4x8) + (4x1) = 44

28 – Fortune

29 – 98
35 men losers, 20 women losers, 17 men double losers, 7 women double losers, 19 mixed double losers.

30 – C
In each row, add together elements of the left and central circles to give the right hand circle. Identical elements cancel each other out.

SOLUTIONS

SECTION 4

1 – Liberal 3385, Socialist 2636, Conservative 2524 and Independent 924.
Add the sum of the three majorities to the total poll of 9469 i.e. 9469 + 749 + 861 + 2461 = 13540, then divide by 4 = 3385. This gives the total number of votes for Liberal.

2 – 4
The number in the centre is the average of the numbers round the outside of each circle.

3 – B
Start top left and move along the top row, then back along the second row etc., in the sequence AKJTL.

4 – Credence, Disbelief

5 – 26 mins

6 – Rhombus
All the others are types of triangle.

7 – 15
$97 \times 8 \div 2 = 388$, $38 \times 8 \div 2 = 152$
$15 \times 2 \div 2 = 15$

8 – 1174 pages

9 – B
First add a dot horizontally, then vertically etc.

10 – Warren

11 – OH
O is midway between I and U
H is midway between K and E

12 – 13
In each line the largest number is the sum of the other three numbers.

13 – Latent, Lurking

14 – 16
$(7 + 10 + 8) - (4 + 4 + 1)$

15 – D
7 - 43 - 259
$7 \times 6 + 1 = 43$
$43 \times 6 + 1 = 259$

16 – He is in a hotel, and is unable to sleep because the man in the adjoining room is snoring loudly. His telephone call wakes the snorer and he is, therefore, able to get to sleep.

17 – 72
$24 \times 4 = 96$, $13 \times 4 = 52$, $14 \times 4 = 56$, $17 \times 4 = 68$, $19 \times 4 = 76$

18 – E

19 – L
Add the numbers $5 + 4 + 6 = 15$. L is the fifteenth letter from the end of the alphabet.

20 – 3
Opposite numbers total 15.

21 – D

22 – D

23 – 180
Cats + Dogs + Hamsters = $1/3 + 1/4 + 1/5 = 47/60$
the remainder = $13/60$ = the number of goldfish
if $13/60 = 39$, total number of animals $= (39 \times 60)/13 = 180$

24 – C
Two lower circles combine to produce the circle above, but similar symbols disappear.

25 – D
(4+)

26 – Friday

27 – 36
Multiply the number of lines used to draw each diagram by the number of enclosed areas formed by the lines.

28 – 3
$(5 + 9 + 2 + 4 + 3) - (6 + 8 + 1 + 1 + 4)$

29 – Umbrage, Offence

30 – C

SECTION 5

1 –

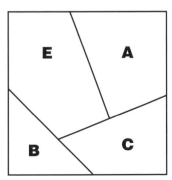

2 – Relate, Impart

3 – 29
The numbers 37529 are being repeated.

4 – Switch J with P
All letters in the left-hand circle are divisible by 4 and in the right by 5, according to their position in the alphabet.

5 – Announce

6 – A triangle

7 – E
The outer figure reduces by one side and goes in the middle, the middle figure increases by one side and goes in the centre. The centre figure increases and goes on the outside.

8 – B
A contains the same numbers as D. And C contains the same numbers as E.

9 – Covet

10 – 30 mph
210 miles at 30 mph = 7 hrs
210 miles at 35 mph = 6 hrs

11 – B
Look across and down, anything common to the first 2 squares is not carried forward to the 3rd square.

12 – 2 : 16
Without the dots it is a cube number. The rest are square numbers.

13 – 111312211X
Each line describes the line above.
1X is followed by 111X
i.e. 1×1 and $1 \times X$

14 – Equilateral
All the others are shapes.

15 – Q

16 – E
There are two sequences running alternately. The first starting with the ellipse increases its number of sides by 1 each time, the second starting with the hexagon decreases by 1 side each time.

17 – 3 kg
$6 \times 4 = 24$, $8 \times 3 = 24$

SOLUTIONS

18 – 23
Alternate prime numbers

19 – Infernal, Demonic

20 – 11

21 – 24
(2 + 16 + 14 + 11) - 19

22 – 30 feet

23 – 38
Subtract numbers in circle B from corresponding numbers in circle A, putting the result in segments of circle C.

24 – $\frac{1}{8000}$

$\frac{1}{20} \times \frac{1}{20} \times \frac{1}{20}$

25 – 2
$\frac{(10 + 11 + 13)}{(8 + 9)}$

26 – 343
Multiply the first two numbers together and divide by two to give the next number along.

27 – 1 Vulpine 2 Pumpkin
3 Pontiff

28 – C

29 – D G
Add together the numerical values of each letter in the words on the left to give a two digit total, and convert each digit to its corresponding letter.

30 – 6
$\frac{12}{4} = 3$ $\frac{14}{7} = 2$ (3 x 2)

SECTION 6

1 –

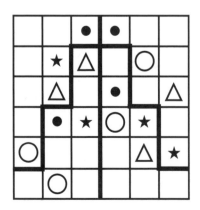

2 – 2
Average = 5, second highest odd number = 7

3 – Elastic, Supple

4 – Z
In each set of pentagons the letters appearing in mirror image positions are two places apart in the alphabet. The bottom letters are two places back from the top.

5 – Venerable

6 – 10
Looking down the first column the numbers are plus 5, down the second column plus 7 and down the third plus 9.

7 – 70

8 – FM
Taking their respective positions in the alphabet all the others when added together total a number divisible by 7.

9 – T
Starting on the left, letters increase in value indicated by the number of pen strokes used to write the letters i.e. A = 1, + 3 strokes = 4 (D), D = 4, + 2 strokes = 6 (F) etc.

10 – E
All the other figures are identical.

11 – 94
The sum of the numbers in each circle is 200.

12 – TY
H(IJ, K(LM)N, O(PQR)S, T(UVWX)Y

13 – 9
Reading anti-clockwise 198 x 2 = 396

14 – Bland

15 – A
The black dot moves anti-clockwise first by one segment then 2, then 3. The white dot moves one place anti-clockwise at each stage.

16 – 620
125 ÷ ¹/₅ = 625 + 5 = 630 - 10 = 620

17 – 3
Each pyramidal group of 3 numbers totals 20.

18 – W
Letters in the top row have 4 lines, in the second row 3 lines and in the bottom row 2 lines.

19 – 422
x 3 + 1, x 3 + 2 etc.

20 – 4 Brothers, 3 Sisters

21 – A
The number of triangles formed increases by 1 each time, i.e. 2, 3, 4, 5.

22 – 80 cents + 20 cents

23 – 444
Number on left reversed minus number on right = top number
1st hexagon: 85 reversed is 58.
58-20 = 38
2nd hexagon: 17 reversed is 71.
71-16 = 55
3rd hexagon: 425 reversed is 524.
524 - 80 = 444

24 – 149
Number at top is reversed and added to the bottom number to produce the second bottom number.
23 + 12 = 44, 44 + 42 = 86, 86 + 63 = 149

25 – 70
2 x 5
6 x 4
12 x 3
20 x 2
$\underline{30 \times 1}$
70

26 – x = $\frac{2}{3}$
$\frac{19 \times 106}{53 \quad 57}$

27 – C

28 – E

29 – E

30 – 71
Numbers connected by lines have the following relationship:
horizontal lines = difference of 10
diagonal lines = difference of 15
vertical lines = difference of 5

SOLUTIONS

SECTION 7

1 – F
In all the others the outer and inner figures are the same.

2 – MU
Working from the top down the left column the sequence is
A(BC)D(EF)G(HI)J(KL)M
Working down the right column the sequence is
A(BCDE)F(GHIJ)K(LMNO)P(QRST)U

3 – Ulterior, Covert

4 – 7
Add the six numbers and divide by 3.

5 – 0
To form a magic square where each horizontal, vertical and corner to corner line totals 12

6 – B
Each mark moves 1 place up in turn.

7 – 3mph
Assume the journey is 6 miles each way. Then at 6mph the outward jog will take 1 hour and the inward crawl 3 hours. This means it takes 4 hours to travel 12 miles, or 1 hour to travel 3 miles.

8 – 7
Starting at 5/4 and working clockwise pairs of numbers in segments increase by 1 each time.

9 – Gatehouse

10 – A
Successive cube numbers reading across, with their middle digit substituted by their respective numbered letter in the alphabet.

11 – E
The piece next to bottom is discarded at each stage.

12 – Triangle = 4.5
Square = 7.2
Diamond = 8.1
Circle = 12.8

13 – 37
Starting at the top of the diagram and moving diagonally down to the right, through groups of three numbers at a time, add together the first two to give the third.

14 – B

15 – 15345
Reverse and add,
8217 + 7128 = 15345

16 – 201
Add 12 and 15 alternately to previous number.

17 – 7
The numbers on each side total 24.

18 – Wrathful, Contented

19 – F

20 – E
In all the others the black circle is at the top.

21 – 312211
The numbers read out the earlier numbers. 1, so one 1 = 11, so two 1's = 21 and so on.

22 – 13 $\frac{3}{4}$
There are 2 sequences +1 $\frac{1}{4}$, -11 $\frac{1}{4}$

23 – 3564
44 × 81

24 – x = $\frac{1}{2}$

$\frac{6 \times 51}{17 \quad 36}$

25 – E

26 – 0
In each square, add the top two numbers together, then multiply by the bottom two numbers in turn to give the value in the centre.

27 – Raillery, Banter

28 – Zero
There were 3 white + 1 black sock.
Chances white pair = $\frac{1}{2}$
mixed pair = $\frac{1}{2}$ — Total = 1
black pair = 0

If there had been 2 white and 2 black socks, then
Chances white pair = $\frac{1}{4}$
mixed pair = $\frac{1}{2}$ — Total = 1
black pair = $\frac{1}{4}$

29 – 42857

30 – The Boston Tea Party, (tea in the sea)

SECTION 8

1 – Hazel
It is brown, the rest are black.

2 – 9
Multiply the numbers on the outside together to obtain the number in the middle, 3 × 3 × 1 × 1 = 9.

3 – 2.4%

4 – 9
Add the number formed by the odd numbers to the number formed by the even numbers,
i.e. 87345 : 84 + 735 = 819,
8 + 19 = 27, 2 + 7 = 9

5 – A
Each arm moves 45° clockwise at each stage.

6 – Guide

7 – Q
Alphabetically it is midway between W and K and N and T.

8 – 1
(9 + 2) - (9 + 1) as in for example the top line where
(9 + 3) - (7 + 2) = 3

9 – Hypothetical, Assumed

10 – 4
(17 + 9) - (8 + 6 + 8)

11 – B
Opposing letters are the same distance apart e.g.
P(QRSTU)V(WXYZA)B, B(C)D(E)F

12 – Sally 171, Jenny 114, Tony 76

13 – 252
The sequence runs × 4, + 3, × 4, + 3 etc.

14 – C
The dot in the inner segment moves anti-clockwise to a different corner at each stage. The other dot alternates between the two outer segments. At each stage the dots change colour; black to white and vice versa.

15 – S
Work along the top line then back along the second etc. There are two sequences running alternately
A(B)C(D)E(F)G(H)I; Y(X)W(V)U(T)S.

SOLUTIONS

16 – 14
Multiply the first 3 numbers and divide by 9.
e.g. 6 x 3 x 7 = 126/9 = 14

17 – A circle

18 – B
So that each connected line of three contains one each of the three symbols.

19 – 3
422 + 436 (x 3) = 2574
719 + 741 (x 3) = 4380

20 – X
Taking their respective numerical value in the alphabet, the top two numbers in each column add up to the bottom number/letter.

21 – x = -25
Order must be taken x, ÷, +, -
-(24) - (18) + 17 = -25

22 – 43
(7 x 6) + 1

23 – 84
In each circle, start with the lowest number and move clockwise. Add the 2-digit number to the sum of its two seperate digits to get the next number in the series,
i.e. 30 + 3 = 33, 33 + 3 + 3 = 39 etc.

24 – T and L
Starting on the left and moving to the right, moving alternately between the top and bottom letter in each pair, one sequence of letters increases in value by 1,2,3,etc. and the other decreases by 1, 2, 3, etc.

25 – 8
Reading from left to right, top row then bottom row, the digits represent the number of letters in each word of the question.

26 – E

27 – A, D

28 – 4
(17 + 18 + 9) - (20 + 20) = 4

29 – 3,185 square yards.
The largest area you can enclose with a single perimeter is a circle. If the circumference is 200, and circumference = 2πr where r = radius of circle and π = 3.14. 200 = 2πr, r = 200/(2 x 3.14) = 31.85 Yards. Area of circle = πr² = 3.14 x (31.85 x 31.85) = 3,185 square yards.

30 – E

SECTION 9

1 – 9lbs

2 – 1
Each block of four numbers totals 20.

3 – FHHE

D	G	H	C	H	E
F	E	(F)	(H)	G	D
H	A	H	F	B	(H)
C	F	E	H	G	F
(E)	G	B	F	C	G
H	D	G	D	G	E

The grid contains 1 x A, 2 x B, 3 x C, 4 x D, 5 x E, 6 x F, 7 x G and 8 x H. The letters are placed so that the same letters are never horizontally or vertically adjacent.

4 – D
G and A have the same symbols reversed as do B and F and C and E.

5 – Evasive, Candid

6 – 9
16 x 9 = 144 $\sqrt{144}$ = 12

7 – 28

8 – A

9 – Triangle = 6.5, Square = 4.2, Diamond = 5.8, Circle = 11.4

10 – Work from A-W omitting every third letter in the alphabet.

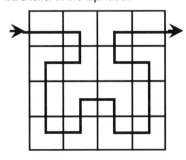

11 – 50mph
40 mph for 80 miles = 2hrs
2hrs @ 50mph = 100 miles

12 – 13.5
The sequence runs x 0.75, x 0.5, x 0.25 repeated.

13 – 7, 1
Each figure shows the number of sides in the two figures adjoining it.

14 – H
In every segment the sum of letters according to their numerical position in the alphabet is 17.

15 – Head

16 – 20:12
Total all the digits each time and add as minutes to arrive at the next time, i.e. 19:49 (1 + 9 + 4 + 9 = 23) + 23mins = 20:12.

17 – 43.75
x 2½

18 – H
Look across each square at letters in the same position. Sequences run:
A(B)C(D)E, Z(YX)W(VU)T, C(DEF)G(HIJ)K, R(QPON)M(LKJI)H

19 – 5
$\sqrt[3]{125}$ = 5

20 – Friday

21 – 9
(14 + 6 + 7) = (9 + 9 + 9)

22 – 121   (Modulo 6)

Modulo 6	Modulo 10
36-6-1	100-10-1
2 - 0 - 0	2 - 0 - 0
8x9=200	8x9=72
7X7=121	7X7=49

23 – Working-Holiday, Pretty-Ugly, Strangely-Familiar, Never-Again, Minor-Miracle, Living-Death

24 – Fluffy

25 – E

26 – Bare minimum

27 – A

28 – π x 26 = 82"

$$\frac{1760 \times 3 \times 12}{82} = 772$$

29 – B

30 – B

SOLUTIONS

1 – 9

2 – Sully

3 – B
In successive rows the four digits total 14, 16, 18, 20, 22.

4 – 6218
7432 = 168 (7 x 4 x 3 x 2), 6198 = 432, 4378 = 672 and 9431 = 108

5 – The pattern follows the path shown. The letters FG in the above grid are the wrong way round.

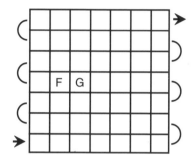

6 – Allow

7 – ATOM (the letters A to M)
– WATER (the letters H to O, i.e. H_2O)

8 – 91
$(14 \times 13) \div 2$

9 – C
The bottom right-hand corner is turned inwards.

10 – Black

11 – 9
The sum in each column is 6, 7, 8, 9.

12 – P
In pentagon 1, J + L = 22
              T + B = 22
In pentagon 2, P + H = 24
              S + E = 24
In pentagon 3, O + K = 26
              J + P = 26

13 – 70 runs
11 innings @ 34 = 374
12 innings @ 32 = 384
                  10

11 innings @ 34 = 374
12 innings @ 37 = 444
                  70

14 – 3/2 or 1.5
If 3x = x + 3, 2x = 3, therefore x = 3/2

15 – 255
Start at 3 and jump to alternate segments in the sequence: (x2 + 1)

16 – Start at R and jump to alternate segments in the sequence: R + 2 = T, T + 3 = W, W + 4 = A, A + 5 = F

17 – 66
Deduct 10, 9, 8, 7

18 – 50mins

19 – 63
Each number describes its position in the grid. 63 = row 6, column 3.

20 – 35
H = 17, D = 6, C = 3, S = 12

21 –

22 – x = -7 ²/₃
Order must be taken x, ÷ , + , -
3 - 2 x 6 + 4 ÷ 3 = x
3 - (12) + (1 ¹/₃) = - 7 ²/₃

23 – 33
(7 x 7) - (14 + 2)

24 – 6.15
Clock times: 9.15, 8.30, 7.45, 7.00, 6.15 (-45m)

25 – A

26 – 7
In each triangle, halve the left hand number, double the right hand number and add together to give the lower number.

27 Mien, Bearing

28 – 7074
Starting on the left, subtract the four seperate digit number to give the next number along.

29 – 2kg
5 x 2 = 10   3 x 4 = 12
3 x 4 = 12   2 x 5 = 10
        22   22

30 – B

1 –

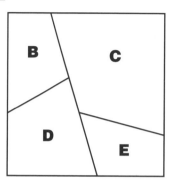

2 – C
In all the others take the position of the first letter of the numberplate, and cube it to obtain the number, e.g. H (8^3) 512.

3 – Follow the route shown to unravel two sequences:
4 (+ 2 + 3 + 4 + 5)
3 (+ 3 + 4 + 5 + 6)

4 – Copy

5 – 9
In each circle, divide the left hand number by 3 and divide the right hand number by 2. Add these values together to give the result at the top of the circle.

6 – D
The pentagon moves anti-clockwise to a different base each time. The dot in the triangle moves clockwise to a different corner each time.

7 – Direct, Meandering

8 – B
So that each line and column totals 17.

9 – 23
(9 + 15) - 1

10 – 12:27
Double the hours each time and add them on as minutes.

11 – C
The bottom large circle contains the same smaller circles as the top large circle but rotated 90°.

SOLUTIONS

12 – Port
It is a general term, the rest being specific landing places.

13 – 5
Each ring contains the digits 1-9 once each only.

14 – 7 @ $1, 3 @ $3, 2 @ $4

15 – 14
The number of straight lines in the four letters

16 – 3
In each line the two three digit numbers added together equal 1000, e.g. 747 + 253 = 1000.

17 – X
20 + 28 = 48 ÷ 2 = 24

18 – 10

19 – 144
x1, x2, x3, x4 repeated

20 – 30
Start at 12 and jump one segment adding the digits (1 + 2) etc.

21 – WHAT
As the instruction for the puzzle is written without a question mark, it is just a statement: "WHAT" replaces the question mark to complete the puzzle!

22 – HER, VICE, ACT, IMP, RUST.

23 – A loses to B   5-4
     B loses to C   5-4
     C loses to A   5-4
It doesn't matter which set of dice they chose, each one has the same chance of winning against the other two.

24 – D   94.25
     H   74.25
     C   41.25
     S   23.25

25 – A

26 – OLD
Take each letter in the first word and replace with the letter that has the reverse alphabetical value, i.e. A becomes Z, B becomes Y etc.

27 – D

28 – Thraldom, Liberty

29 – D
The two circles below form the circle above and similar symbols disappear.

30 – They may have been golfers, but they were playing a game of snooker.

SECTION 12

1 – Joke

2 – B
All the others can be cut out to produce a cube.

3 – P
Taking positions in the alphabet add the letters together and multiply by 2, e.g. A(1) + F(6) = 7 x 2 = 14 (N).

4 – F
Circles are being built up anti-clockwise a quarter of the circumference at a time.

5 – A
A=1, B=2, C=3, these values construct a magic square where each horizontal, vertical and corner to corner line totals 15.

6 – Placid

7 – A
In each row, superimpose the left and right hand diagrams to give the one in the centre.

8 – 15

9 – 29
Start at the top of the diagram and move down to the left in diagonal lines. Numbers in the first line increase by 2 each time, second line by 3, third line by 4 etc.

10 – It was instant coffee and he hadn't yet added water.

11 – 25
8 + 7 + 2 + 4 + 4

12 – $\sqrt{7}$ = 2.646
Square roots 1,2,3,4,5,6,7

13 – 24
Non-prime numbers

14 – 104, 216, 96, 32
78 x 4 = 312 ÷ 3 = 104

15 – 41
Question uses modulo 6
5 x 5 = 25
       = (4 x 6) + (1 x 6) = 41

16 – A
White dots are carried forward when they appear three times in the previous three circles. Black dots are carried forward when they appear once.

17 – 9
6 x 9 = 54   54 - 9 = 45

18 – 47
Looking across and down, each number is the sum of the two previous numbers.

19 – C

20 – 16
Multiply values in the left hand circle by 2 and values in the middle circle by 3. Add together these two values and place the result in the corresponding segment of the right hand circle.

21 – x = $\frac{2}{3}$

$\frac{7}{16}$ x $\frac{32}{21}$

22 – x = -52
7 - 32 - 3 - 24 = -52
Order must be taken x, ÷, +, -

23 – 7
(18 + 12 + 3) - (7 + 9 + 10)

24 – 60°
Remember this is a cube.

25 – Triangle = - 4.2
     Square = 11.5
     Diamond = -1.8
     Circle = 6.6

26 – 204
Converting modulo 9 to modulo 10,
     45   = (4 x 9) + 5
          = 41
     148 = (1 x 81) + (4 x 9) + 8
          = 125
41 = 125   = 166, in modulo 9,
166   = (2 x 81) + (0 x 9) + 4
          = 2   0   4

SOLUTIONS

27 – 18
In each column of the table, calculate the difference in alphabetical values of the two letters and multiply by 2 to give the numerical value at the bottom.

28 – 231
Converting modulo 4 to modulo 10,
$\quad$ 21 $\quad$ = (2 x 4) + 1 = 9
$\quad$ 11 $\quad$ = (1 x 4) + 1 = 5
9 x 5 = 45, converting 45 to modulo 4, $\quad$ 45 $\quad$ = (2 x 16) + (3 x 4) + 1
$\qquad\qquad$ = 2 $\quad$ 3 $\quad$ 1

29 – E

30 – The odds favour the dealer. After picking one card of a particular colour, the odds of picking a second one of the same colour are 4:9, which is slightly under evens.

SECTION 13

1 – B
At each stage the circle moves two forward one back, the dot two back one forward, the white triangle two back one forward and the black triangle one forward two back.

2 – A, D, H, E, G, C, F, B

3 – 481
They are square numbers, 1, 4, 9, 16, 25, 36, 49, 64, 81, split into groups of 3.

4 – Glitzy

5 – B
Start at the top and move the opposite arrow 90° anti-clockwise, then move opposite arrows clockwise, anti-clockwise etc. in following segments.

6 – Rotate anti-clockwise +1

7	2	6
5	9	4
8	3	5

7 – 194, 120; 2 + 6 = 8, 2 + 8 = 10 etc.

8 – Craven

9 – 9
9 + 85 + 947 = 1041

10 – 30 mins
20 miles @ 40 mph = 30 mins
30 mins @ 60 mph = 30 miles

11 – 9
8 + 9 = 8 + 3 + 6

12 – B
Carry curves forward from the first two squares to the final square in each line and column, except where two curves appear in the same position, in which case they are cancelled out.

13 – J
In opposite segments letter + number = 20, e.g. M(13) + 7 = 20.

14 – Tall

15 – 36 mins

16 – B
Straight lines turn to curves and vice versa.

17 – 7430
Multiply the second and last digits and add, 4 x 0 = 0, therefore 7430 + 0 = 7430.

18 – IO
There are two sequences:
A(B)C(D)E(F)G(H)I and
C(DE)F(GH)I(JK)L(MN)O

19 – 9
The single numbers in the first circle are the sum of the 2 figure digits in the second circle and vice versa.

20 – B
The ends of the lines terminate at the corner points of the pentagon.

21 – 6

22 – Witch doctor

23 – E
All letters use straight lines.

24 – Set both timers off together. When the five minute timer has run out, three minutes remain in the other.

25 – 21

26 – A

27 – A is a Truer; **B** is a Fibber; **C** is a Truer.

28 – D
A is the same as F
B is the same as G
C is the same as E

29 – C

30 – D

SECTION 14

1 – J
Taking their numerical position in the alphabet, the middle letter is the average of the other 6.

2 – Apathy

3 – 3472
A B C D $\qquad$ A + B = C
1 4 5 9 $\qquad$ B + C = D

4 – D
In all the others the total number of sides in the two figures equals 11.

5 – 7
To his wife 3.5 + 0.5 = 4
To my wife 1.5 + 0.5 = 2
To me 0.5 + 0.5 = 1

6 – C
In each shape, add the two right hand numbers together to give the top left number, and add the top centre and right hand numbers to give the lower left number.

7 – Cringe

8 – 9

9 – 23

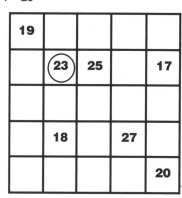

10 – RGC
Reverse 379 i.e. 973, R is ninth from the end of the alphabet GC are seventh and third from the beginning.

SOLUTIONS

11 – Grassland

12 – A
Dots are only carried forward to the end square when they appear in the same position in the two preceding squares looking both across and down.

13 – 8
Add 82 + 65 + 68 + 93 = 308 among 100 ladies. This gives 3 items to each and 4 items to 8 ladies. The least number of ladies to have had all 4 items is, therefore, 8.

14 – 52173
The numbers swap places as in the first two sets.

15 – Pepper

16 – 771
Reverse second number and add to first, thus 184 (481 reversed) = 771.

17 – C

18 – 646 + 6 = 652

19 – 6
Straight lines minus curved lines

20 – 9286
In the others multiply the first and last digits and divide by 2 to obtain the middle digit/s.

21 – A 15   B 12   C 14   D 13   E 11

22 – 3D
Draw a vertical line with 4 people on left and 4 people on right and find centre. Draw a horizontal line with 4 people on the top and 4 people on the bottom and find centre. Both lines should meet at 3D.

23 – 620
Converting modulo 7 to modulo 10,
31 = (3 × 7) + 1   = 22
20 = (2 × 7)   = 14
14 × 22 = 308, converting 308 to modulo 7,
308   = (6 × 49) + (2 × 7) + 0
   = 6   2   0

24 – Ten of Diamonds
Start at the top left of the diagram and move to the right, then down one row and to the left etc. The value of each card increases by 3, then 4, then 5. Each row and column contains one card from each suit.

25 – 1110
Converting modulo 2 (also called binary) to modulo 10,
10 = (1 × 2) + 0 = 2 and 100 = (1 × 4) + (0 × 2) + 0 = 4
101 = (1 × 4) + (0 × 2) + 1 = 5
and 1001 = (1 × 8) + (0 × 4) + (0 × 2) + 1 = 9
9 + 5 = 14, converting 14 to modulo 2,
14   = (1 × 8) + (1 × 4) + (1 × 2) + 0
   = 1   1   1   0

26 – Seraphic, Celestial

27 – A

28 –

In each row or column, the men have no hat, a single peaked hat or a double peaked hat, shaded alternately black and white. They also have arms to the left, arms on both sides or arms to the right in a similar, alternate fashion.

29 – 46
17 − 16 + 51 − 6 = 46

30 – U
In each circle, start with the letter in the centre on the left hand side and move clockwise. Letters increase in value by 5 each time for circle A, 7 each time for circle B and 9 each time for circle C.

SECTION 15

1 – B
At each stage the small white circle moves 2 segments clockwise, the large black circle moves one clockwise, the large white circle moves two places clockwise and the small black circle moves two places anti-clockwise.

2 – 11.28
37 minutes is added at each stage.

3 – 1 min 12 seconds
Time = (1.25 + 0.25) × $\frac{60}{75}$ mins
= 1.5 × $\frac{60}{75}$ = 1.2 mins (1 min 12 secs)

4 – 11
Each number describes the empty spaces before and after it in the row. 11 should go on the bottom row, 2nd from the left.

5 – A
So that one each of the three different symbols appears in each row and column.

6 – Brisk

7 – PK
Add the alphabetical numerical value of each of the four outside letters. The centre circle contains the numbered letter counting from the front of the alphabet and back from the end.

8 – 3
86/2 = 43

9 – Diligent, Indifferent

10 – 15

11 – across: 121, 64, 169, 25, 49
down: 196, 81, 324, 36, 361

12 – 3
6 × 5 = 30   5 × 9 = 45
3 × 8 = 24   3 × 3 = 9
   54   54

13 – 7 empty seats
13 people paid $3.79 each.

14 – 121
Converting modulo 5 to modulo 10,
14   = (1 × 5) + 4 = 9
4   = 4
9 × 4 = 36, converting 36 to modulo 5,
36   = (1 × 25) + (2 × 5) + 1
   = 1   2   1

15 – D
The letters and numbers occupy alternate lines and move along from left to right then back on their next row right to left etc., in the sequence; numbers 48321; letters GPXNQ.

16 – Amazing

17 – 3
The sum of each pair of numbers reading across and down is one more than the previous pair of numbers, e.g. 3 + 2 = 5, 5 + 1 = 6.

SOLUTIONS

18 – 12
In each circle, add the two upper numbers together, multiply the sum by 3 and divide by 2 to give the value at the bottom.

19 – R
Start at A and move clockwise first omitting one letter then two;
A(B)C(DE)F(G)H(IJ)K(L)M(NO)P(Q)R

20 – 15 minutes

21 – 10 ¼
There are 2 series +7 ¾, -5 ¼

22 – 17 ½ mph
Against wind   15 mph
With wind   20 mph
Wind =   2 ½ mph

23 – K
All straight lines. Letters in order of the alphabet.

24 – 1.115"
Hand moves 216°
$\frac{360}{216} \times 4.2" = 7"$

$\frac{7"}{2 \times \pi} = 1.115"$

25 – 7 or 23
Reading downwards 3 small numbers = 1 large number

26 – $920
Servant's wages = $1000
Car's value = $920
He's working for $1920 ($1000 + $920) per year. He only works for 7 months, therefore the only wages he is entitled to is:
$\frac{7}{12} \times \$1920 = \$1120$
As they've given him the car, worth $920, they have to hand him $200 cash.

27 – 1, -1, 2, -2, 3

28 – B

29 – E

30 – Four of Hearts
In each row, add up the values of the red cards, and subtract the total of the black cards to give the value of the card to the right.

SECTION 16

1 –

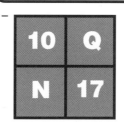

Look across at identical segments. There are four sequences:
4, 6, 8, 10; H(IJ)K(LM)N(OP)Q; B(CDE)F(GHI)J(KLM)N; 8, 11, 14, 17

2 – 61, 77, 27, 41; 7 x 4 = 28 : reverse = 82, 8 x 2 = 16: reverse = 61

3 – Stampede

4 – 2
Start at the first one and jump to alternate segments clockwise in the sequence x1, x2, x3, etc.

5 – C
The dot in the top left quarter moves one corner anti-clockwise, in the top right quarter the dot moves backwards and forwards between two corners, in the bottom right the dot moves backwards and forwards between two corners, and in the bottom left it moves one corner anti-clockwise.

6 – Add digits of 2 to obtain 1
Add digits of 1 to obtain 4
Multiply digits of 2 to obtain 3
Multiply digits of 3 to obtain 5

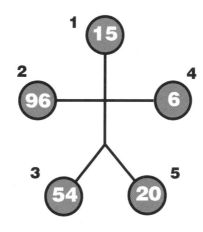

7 – Crusade, Campaign

8 – Visit the squares in the following order:

13	23	17	7	11
18	8	12	3	22
21	2	6	10	16
9	14	19	T	4
1	20	15	5	24

9 – 3:19
The difference between opposite times is less 20 mins right to left

10 – D
The medium size rectangle is moving one place from left to right at each stage.

11 – 84
$^{42}/_3 \times 6$

12 – Twelve

13 – Work from Z to A in the sequence ZYX then omit three letters (WVU) TSR etc, following the route shown:

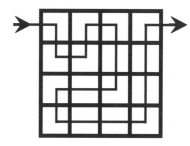

14 – G
In all the others only sections formed by the intersection of two circles are shaded.

15 – 6
69382/2 = 34691

16 – 25 minutes

17 – Momentary, Permanent

18 – 63
Add sum of digits x2 each time.

19 – To the number 4 also
In successive faces multiply the numbers the hands are pointing to, to obtain the sequence 24, 22, 20, 18, 16.

20 – 16, 24
To complete a list of factors of the final number, 96.

SOLUTIONS

21 – STVU

22 – 4

23 – Hurricane

24 – B

25 – A

26 – B

27 – C
The lower circles add together to form the circle above and only similar symbols go up.

28 – G
A is the same as F
B is the same as E
C is the same as D

29 – Turbid

30 – B, D

SECTION 17

1 – B
The missing dot moves three places, then four etc. When reaching the end of the arc it starts again at the beginning.

2 – 4
The columns added increase in the sequence 10, 13, 16, 19.

3 – Z, P
There are two sequences reading diagonally:
A, B (C)D(EF)G(HIJ)K(LMNO)P and
K(LMNO)P(QRS)T(UV)W(X)YZ

4 – Ape-like

5 – B
Each horizontal and vertical line contains one each of the three symbols. In each horizontal and vertical line one of the symbols points in a different direction.

6 – 7, 21, 22

7 – Z

8 – 6
1079 - 93 = 986

9 –
```
    1365
 x   407
    9555
   5460 ..
  555555
```

10 – 54 appears twice and 26 is missing

11 – Lavish

12 – 81015
7 + 1 = 8, 1 + 9 = 10, 9 + 6 = 15

13 – 35% of Diameter

14 – 10 miles
The man walks 5 miles at 4 mph and so takes 1 $\frac{1}{4}$ hours. Therefore, the dog runs 1 $\frac{1}{4}$ hours at 8 mph and thus covers 10 miles.

15 – 10
20 x 5 = 100 $\sqrt{100}$ = 10,
18 + 22 = 40/4 = 10

16 – Serene

17 – 14

18 – B
For each single number, D is A plus 1; E is C plus 1.

19 – 71
Arrange the digits 396 in every possible way and divide each resultant number by 9 to obtain the other numbers:
396/9 = 44, 369/9 = 41
936/9 = 104, 963/9 = 107
639/9 = 71, 693/9 = 77

20 – Sheep $20, pig $40

21 – A

22 – C, F

23 – A

24 – Assuage, Aggravate

25 – E

26 – D

27 –

Insects	Birds	Animals
Woodlice	Hornbill	Aardvark
Emmet	Perchary	Bushbaby
Slug	Shelduck	Cachalot
Moth	Fulmar	Panda

28 – C

29 – Ill-Health   Non-Dairy Creamer
    Night Light   Even Odds
    Idiot Savant   Homeless Shelter

30 – 27, 25, 18, 16, 14

SECTION 18

1 – A
The diamond moves down one at each stage and rotates 90° at each stage. When it gets to the bottom it starts at the top again at the next stage.

2 – 14
Add successive square numbers (1, 4, 9, 16, 25) at each stage.

3 – 2500 sq yds
50 x 50, the square providing the greatest area

4 – 3 stages

5 – 84
84 - 12 ÷ 3 = 24

6 – D
A quarter of the length inclines 45° at each stage. Once a section has inclined it keeps inclining a further 45° at each stage.

7 – 128
Reverse each number and add to produce the number in the centre i.e. 61 + 41 + 26 = 128.

8 – Magistrate

9 – 7
In opposite segments 4 x 4 = 2 x 8, 7 x 4 = 2 x 14 etc.

10 – 6436
6 x 6 = 36, 8 x 8 = 64

11 – A
The vertical lines move inwards then the horizontal lines up and down at each stage alternately.

12 – B
They are the numbers 2, 4, 6, 8 displayed digitally but each with a missing section.

13 – L
Add the numerical values of the three corner letters and then take the Roman numeral equally the total; 17 + 24 + 9 = 50 (L)

14 – Oar

15 – A
The ellipse rotates 90° and goes inside the pentagon which rotates 180°. The diamond rotates 90° and goes underneath the others.

SOLUTIONS

16 – 3
Add the digits $4 + 1 + 1 + 3 = 9$ and take square root.

17 – 3 to 1
Each car to come out of the testing area has an even chance of being blue or white i.e. 1 in 2 to power 3. The repeat 3 times is 1 in 2 or 8. However, as the 1st car will always be blue or white, only another 2 cars of the same colour are required to complete a sequence of 3 blue or 3 white. The chances are, therefore, 2^2 = 4 or 3 to 1.

18 – D
In the others the minutes are the difference between the hours and seconds.

19 – F
In the others eyes right, curl left; eyes left, curl right; squint, curl straight up.

20 –

The numbers 147683 start bottom left and travel up the first column, then back down the second etc.

21 – 9
1st diamond $\frac{6}{2} = 3$, $\frac{27}{3} = 9$, $\frac{18}{9} = 2$

2nd diamond $\frac{8}{4} = 2$, $\frac{2}{2} = 1$, $\frac{13}{1} = 13$

3rd diamond $\frac{18}{9} = 2$, $\frac{10}{2} = 5$, $\frac{45}{5} = 9$

4th diamond $\frac{10}{5} = 2$, $\frac{8}{2} = 4$, $\frac{20}{4} = 5$

22 – $\frac{117}{169} = \frac{9}{13}$

23 – Pin-Cushion   Church-Mouse
Brandy-Snaps   Chimney-Sweep
Stale-Mate   Fox Hounds

24 – D

25 – Limpid, Pellucid

26 – 16061

---

27 – 120
1x, 2x, 3x, 4x, 5x, 6x, 7x, 8x, starting at 1
1 - 2 - 6 - 24 - 120 - 720 - 5040 - 40320
Jump 2 quadrants

28 – $\frac{3}{8} \div \frac{15}{24} = \frac{3}{8} \times \frac{24}{15} = \frac{3}{5}$

29 – 72

30 – C

SECTION 19

1 – D
The dot alternates between the two positions and alternates black/white, the square moves one side clock-wise, alternative white/black and inside/outside ellipse, the small ellipse does the same anti-clockwise and the star moves round the inside of the ellipse alternating black/white.

2 – Trombone

3 – 8
$(7 \times 8) + 2 = 58$

4 – 5191
$16 + 35 = 51$, $68 + 23 = 91$

5 – It was a convertible car and the top was down. He was shot through the open top.

6 – D
The sequence runs circle, triangle, ellipse and the shading runs horizontal then vertical stripes.

7 – Trumpet
It is blown, the rest are string.

8 – 9
$5732 - 3926 = 1806$

9 – O
Opposite segments contain letters an equal distance from the beginning and end of the alphabet.

10 – Limpid

11 – F
The figures are being repeated with the left-hand only shown.

12 – Wanton

13 – 16
$7 \times 4 = 28$, $6 \times 2 = 12$, $28 - 12 = 16$

---

14 – 960
480×2

15 – Pottery

16 – D
The black square in the top row moves right to left. In the second row it moves left to right. In the third row it moves right to left. In the fourth row it moves left to right at each stage.

17 –

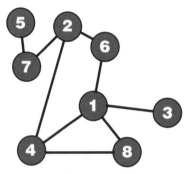

18 – D
The contents of each circle are determined by the two circles directly below it. H + D = S, D + S = H, S + C = D, S + H = C, therefore the top figure diamonds follows clubs + spades.

19 – 33
$3 \times 2 + 1 = 7$, $7 \times 3 + 5 = 26$, $4 \times 4 + 9 = 25$ and $6 \times 5 + 3 = 33$

20 – $568.43 + 12.9 + 168.72 + 563.8 = 1313.85$

21 – Garden-Gnome   Ocean-Liner
Wishing-Well   Lucky-Charm
Staff-Car   Board-Walk

22 – Insidious, Disingenuous

23 – A

24 – Backward glance

25 – 10
$(25 - x) + x + (20 - x) + 5 = 40$
$50 - x = 40$
$x = 10$

26 – 3
Outer number + Inner opposite = same as Inner number + Outer opposite

27 – $\frac{7}{8} \times \frac{64}{49} = 1\frac{1}{7}$

28 – Candle-Grease   Hat-Stand
Tap-Dance   Picture-Frame
Ginger-Beer   Foot-Loose

SOLUTIONS

29 – Fain, Unwilling

30 – B

SECTION 20

1 – C
There are two alternate sequences of arrows each rotating 45° clockwise at each stage and turning white/black and vice versa at each stage.

2 – 13
$\sqrt{36} + \sqrt{49}$, i.e. 6 + 7 = 13

3 – 3
+2, -1, +2 etc.

4 – Pray, Beseech

5 – 14
The left-hand circle contains the sum of each combination of circled numbers from the right-hand circle and vice versa.

6 – E
A and C are the same with black/white reversal, as are B/G, D/H and F/I

7 – 48
Multiply then add alternate digits i.e.
7 x 9 = 63 + 3 = 66 x 5 = 330 + 8 = 338 x 2 = 676,
6 x 7 = 42 + 6 = 48

8 – 4
Work along the top row, then back along the second row after starting at the top left-hand corner square. Add digits then add again e.g. 9 + 7 = 16 and 1 + 6 = 7

9 – Swimming
All the other sports use a ball

10 – E
Each row and column contains one each of the three symbols and one each of the different slanting lines.

11 – 3
Looking down, mirror image groups of three numbers total the same e.g. 661 + 98 + 7 = 3 + 39 + 724

12 – 336, 378, 168, 210
3 x 8 x 7 x 2 = 336, 3 x 3 x 6 = 54

13 – 24
There are two sequences starting at the two numbers 25. Jump to alternate segments in the sequences: 25, 26, 27, 28 and 25, 24, 23, 22.

14 – C
The vertical stripe moves left to right at each stage, the horizontal stripe moves top to bottom. The dot at the left-hand bottom corner initially moves diagonally upwards. The other dot, at the right-hand bottom corner initially moves diagonally downwards. Whenever a stripe or dot reaches the end of their row they start again from the opposite end at the next stage.

15 –

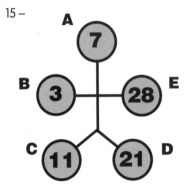

A x B = D
D + A = E
(A + E) - (B + D) = C

16 – 14, 19
Add digits, 8 + 6 = 14, 8 + 6 + 1 + 4 = 19

17 – A
Dots are only transferred to the middle circle when they appear in the same position in three of the outer circles.

18 – Man 'A' again wins.
We know from the first race that man 'A' runs 100 metres at the same time that man 'B' runs 95 metres. It follows, therefore, that as man 'A' starts 5 metres behind the line, the men will be dead level at 5 metres short of the winning line. As man 'A' is the faster runner, he goes on to overtake man 'B' in the last 5 metres and win the race.

19 – 9
Multiply two inside numbers and divide by four to find outside number.
e.g. 4 x 9 = 36/4 = 9, 8 x 3 = 24/4 = 6

20 – Animals

21 – Abalone (A . B - ALONE)

22 – A $^4/_7$
    B $^2/_7$
    C $^1/_7$

23 – Eddie

24 – 3   Cylinder
    2   Sphere
    1   Cone

25 – Q
All rounded letters starting at B

26 – Parlour-Maid   Steam-Train
    Penny-Whistle   Chain-Gang
    Cup-Hook   Teddy-Bear

27 – Derogate, Appreciate

28 – C

29 – $\frac{19}{26} \times \frac{52}{38} = 1$

30 –   285
     39
   2565
    855
  11115